NORBERT SZÁMVÉBER

COMBAT HISTORY
OF THE
PANZER-ABTEILUNG 103
SEPTEMBER 1943 – AUGUST 1944

peko PUBLISHING

Norbert Számvéber
COMBAT HISTORY OF THE PANZER-ABTEILUNG 103
SEPTEMBER 1943 – AUGUST 1944

PUBLISHED BY
PeKo Publishing Kft.
H-8360 Keszthely, Bessenyei György utca 37.
Email: info@pekobooks.com
Website: www.pekobooks.com
Facebook: www.facebook.com/PeKoPublishing

AUTHOR Norbert Számvéber
EDITED BY Derik Hammond
TRANSLATED BY Tímea Tóthné Vágó
COVER DESIGNED BY Ádám Nagy [www.nadam.hu]
PHOTOS Péter Kocsis, National Archives

FIRST PUBLISHED 2016

ISBN 978-615-5583-01-8

PRINT Kvadrát Print [www.kvadratprint.hu]

Table of Contents

Introduction 7

Re-establishment of the German *Panzer-Abteilung 103* and its transport to Italy *9*

Italy pulls out of the war 20

Fighting from Salerno to the River Volturno 27

In the "Bernhardt Line" 52

Against the Anzio bridgehead in the area of Aprilia 68

Holding manoeuvres up to the River Arno 114

Introduction

Unfortunately very few German unit war diaries from WW2, especially those written by elements under divisional level, survived. However, such documents give a particular insight into the most intriguing details of combat actions. Nevertheless, PeKo Publishing House managed to find itself in possession of such a rarity, the *Kriegstagebuch* of *Panzer-Abteilung 103,* which covers the period from summer 1943 to spring 1944. I was more than glad to undertake the task of writing a combat history of the unit based on that war diary, supplemented by other contemporary sources.

Reading the documents relating to the history of this armoured unit, which was compelled to engage in combat with Allied troops using StuG. III assault guns instead of tanks on a terrain in Italy where the conditions were much less than ideal for armoured tactics, was illuminating. Most of the time, *Panzer-Abteilung 103* was put into action while broken up into platoon or company strength units at best which were then simultaneously deployed at several locations to provide support for German infantry or to fight against the Allies' armoured fighting vehicles.

Regrettably, the *Abteilung's* diary ends in April 1944 with its appendices only partially intact. Despite this, a very detailed picture emerges of the significant role played by *Panzer-Abteilung 103* at a time when Italy pulled out of the war and the Allies landed at Salerno and during the fighting at the Anzio/Nettuno.

Vienna, April 2016

1

Re-establishment of the German *Panzer-Abteilung 103* and its transport to Italy

Panzer-Abteilung 103 (103rd Armoured Battalion) was one of the German *3. Infanterie-Division (mot.)*'s (3rd Motorized Infantry Division) units with significant firepower. Certain elements of the *6. Armee,* destroyed during the Battle of Stalingrad, were re-established in spring 1943, including the *3. Infanterie-Division (mot.)*[1] with *Panzer-Abteilung 103* in its order of battle.

The armoured unit was formed on 1 March 1943 in France by the redesignation of *Panzer-Abteilung 386.* Its strength was made up by soldiers of the annihilated *Panzer-Abteilung 103* returned to the hinterland as well as veterans from the North-African theatre.

Panzer-Abteilung 103 was stationed in southern France until early July, then relocated to the area of Lyon between 10 and 13 June.

As a result of the ongoing reorganizations in the German war industry, the unit was equipped with *Sturmgeschütz* (abbr. StuG.) III assault guns without turret instead of the tried-and-tested Panzer III and Panzer IV tanks.[2]

The 42 assault guns issued on 15 June 1943 were distributed as follows:

- staff (and staff company) with two assault guns;
- *1. Kompanie* with 10 assault guns
- *2. Kompanie* with 10 assault guns;
- *3. Kompanie* with 10 assault guns;
- *4. Kompanie* with 10 assault guns.[3]

1 The new division was formed as *3. Panzergrenadier-Division,* by the redesignation of *386. Infanterie-Division (mot.)* in March 1943. The units belonging to its order of battle took over the designation numbers of the corresponding units of *3. Infanterie-Division (mot.). See* Dieckhoff, Gerhard: *3. Infanterie-Division – 3. Infanterie-Division (mot.) – 3. Panzergrenadier-Division* Cuxhaven, s.a., p. 243.

2 Since no *Panzerjäger-Abteilung* was attached to the *3. Panzergrenadier-Division* until late summer 1944, the assault guns of *Panzer-Abteilung 103* represented the only mobile and armoured AT fire-power of the division during the fighting in Italy. *See* Dieckhoff, Gerhard: *3. Infanterie-Division – 3. Infanterie-Division (mot.) – 3. Panzergrenadier-Division* Cuxhaven, s.a., p. 244.

3 *Kriegstagebuch der Panzer-Abteilung 103* (copy in author's possession), p. 1. Unless otherwise indicated, this document was used as the main primary source for the period between early June 1943 and late April 1944.

On 20 June, *Hauptmann* Rudolf Haen arrived and assumed command of *Panzer-Abteilung 103.* Previously he had been the commander of the *1. Kompanie* of the destroyed unit.[4] The former battalion commander, *Hauptmann* Ewald von Stünzner,[5] had been transferred to the *34. Infanterie-Division* fighting in the Eastern Theatre.

On 25 and 26 June, one Panzer III tank, five cars, nine motorcycles and a low-loader trailer from *Panzer-Abteilung 103* participated in the military exercises held by the division. Their aim was to check the mobility of the troops while using their heaviest and longest vehicles in hardly passable mountainous areas.

Simultaneously with those exercises, *Panzer-Abteilung 103* was ordered to relocate again.

On 27 June, at 0200 hours, some of the soldiers previously assigned to this task entrained at Lyon-Perrache railway station. During the day orders were received to regroup the remaining bulk of the unit.

At the same time *Panzer-Abteilung 103* was ordered to leave behind the AFVs 'inherited' from *Panzer-Abteilung 386* – except for three command combat vehicles – in assigned quarters in the area of Montluel. Those AFV's were to have been taken over by another unit arriving there soon. To carry out the task, the AFVs were assembled in the area of the Montluel ammunition dump. For that purpose, the unit left a handover detachment of 50 soldiers behind.[6]

SS-units attached to *Panzer-Abteilung 103* were placed under the direct command of the division on 27 June.

During the march from the offload stations to their new quartering areas in San Lorenzo and Acquapendente, Italy,[7] every motor vehicle of the unit was exposed to excessive wear and tear. Soon different mechanical failures occurred in the assault guns due to material defects and as a consequence of probable production sabotage. By way of illustration of the latter, a piece of sandpaper was found inside the crankcase of one of the StuG. IIIs. A number of failures were detected in the wheeled vehicles, most of which were rather old.

As a result, having arrived in their new quartering area, the troops performed exclusively maintenance tasks. During their first major march, the battalion became aware of the difficulties to be expected on a long march 'on foot'. Rapid and complete supply seemed uncertain. The situation concerning the motor vehicles demanded a solution as the unit had to carry five allowances of fuel plus 106 shells per assault gun with them. However, StuG. IIIs couldn't be loaded in the same way as the tanks had been earlier. But, by means of partly rearranging the interior of the fighting compartment of the assault guns, the number of shells loaded could be increased from 54 to 71 without imposing any restrictions whatsoever on the crew.

---

4 The *1. Kompanie* of *Panzer-Abteilung 103* under the command of *Hauptmann* Haen knocked out 22 AFVs during the elimination of a Soviet penetration in the area of Borodkin, north-west of Stalingrad, 18 September 1942. The AFV of the company commander, who was always leading from the front, was fired on by six Soviet AFVs from their semi-covered firing positions. One of them was knocked out by Haen's AFV but the German combat vehicle also received a hit during the fight, and caught fire. Having suffered severe burns, the captain changed combat vehicles and continued to lead his AFVs in action until the penetration was eliminated by them. His company knocked out a total of 88 Soviet AFVs in July–September 1942, including 15 kills scored by the AFV of the company commander. On 12 December 1942, Haen was awarded the Knight's Cross of the German Iron Cross.

5 Stünzner, as commander of the *3. Kompanie* of *Panzer-Abteilung 103*, was awarded the Knight's Cross of the German Iron Cross on 10 September 1942.

6 *Kriegstagebuch der Panzer-Abteilung 103* (copy in author's possession), p. 3.

7 Dieckhoff, Gerhard: *3. Infanterie-Division – 3. Infanterie-Division (mot.) – 3. Panzergrenadier-Division* Cuxhaven, s.a., p. 245.

Having reorganized its transport capacity, *Panzer-Abteilung 103* – although with minor restrictions – became operational.[8]

On 1 July, *Hauptmann* Haen was appointed commander of *Panzer-Abteilung 103.* With him arrived *Oberleutnant* Arno Fischer, who became commander of the *4. Kompanie. Leutnant* Walz was appointed as the commander of the supply column in the staff company.

On 6 July, a total of four *Unteroffiziere* set off from the *2., 3.* and *4. Kompanien* to the replacement unit to attend the 13th training course for cadets.

A day later, in accordance with a divisional command, *Hauptmann* Fritz Heller travelled to the *Führerhauptquartier* (Hitler's HQ) to arrange for some sort of measures to be taken to resolve the dire situation regarding the unit's vehicles.

From 12 July, training continued. Its focal point was to familiarize every soldier in the unit with the combat vehicles – the assault guns – with which they were still unfamiliar. Tactics, which were slightly different from those used by tanks, were to be adjusted to suit the new weaponry.

On 14 July, the commander of the unit, *Hauptmann* Haen, issued special orders regarding training and the assignment of the supply column during deployment as well as specifying reporting rules. As regards the training drill carried out during the previous week, he was basically satisfied but he also expressed the opinion that discipline should be improved. Gunnery practice with the assault guns' 7.5cm cannons at ranges up to 800m proved unsuccessful. Cooperation between the driver and the gunner had to be practised continuously. The assault gun commanders were urged to improve their range-estimation skills. Crews of the assault guns had to practise changing firing positions quickly as well as locking on to fast-moving targets.[9]

On 15 July, supernumeraries (77 men) of the unit were ordered to *Panzer-Ersatz und Ausbildungs-Abteilung 10* in Zinten, East-Prussia.

On 16 July, *Hauptmann* Heller returned from the *Führerhauptquartier* and it became evident from his report that the unit could not expect the arrival of new vehicles for the time being.

On 17 July, *Panzer-Abteilung 103* executed another exercise including LFX (live fire exercises) on the shore of Lake Bolsena. Here, for the first time, all the companies of the unit were employed together as a whole. Individual companies had already carried out gunnery practice in the area of the lake a week before. During this exercise however, they could practice combined arms cooperation together with a company of *Panzer-Aufklärungs-Abteilung 103* and a battery of *Artillerie-Regiment (mot.) 3.* The exercise was inspected by *Generalleutnant* Fritz-Hubert Gräser, commander of the *3. Panzergrenadier-Division* and also the Italian brigadier general Gaetano Marzoli.

As part of the exercise the unit performed a marching exercise, during which troops gave evidence of their good marching discipline. While on the move, it became evident that the march could be strongly hindered by detours made around tilled areas and other privately owned lands. Therefore, after leaving San Lorenzo and heading towards the sea, crowding became more frequent, and it was to be avoided during action. Passing through forested areas

8 *Kriegstagebuch der Panzer-Abteilung 103* (copy in author's possession), p. 4.

9 *Kriegstagebuch der Panzer-Abteilung 103* (copy in author's possession), p. 8.

– a task difficult even for tanks – was extremely disadvantageous because an assault gun, which did not have a traversing gun turret, could block the road to their own forces marching up from behind when taking up a firing position. It also turned out that in wooded areas and hardly passable terrain, the assault guns could only operate with strong infantry support, otherwise they might suffer significant losses.

It also became evident that the side-skirting providing protection to sides of the hulls of the StuG. III combat vehicles could easily fall away on rough terrain. Moreover, they could get stuck between the road wheels and throw off the track.

The extremely poor hit rate for the HE (hollow charge) shells might have been due to the fact that there were no appropriate aiming marks for this type of ammunition in the telescopic sights of the assault guns. Therefore reservations about this type of ammunition held by veterans with experience gained in the Eastern Front, were reinforced.[10]

On 21 and 22 July, the division's theatrical group visited the unit and their performance was highly appreciated by all.

From 25 July, in accordance with an order of the division, each and every soldier was expected to participate more intensively in athletic activities and various sports competitions.

On the same day, orders were received to reorganize the Pz.-Abt. 103's order of battle. From then on the unit, equipped with assault guns, possessed a total of 42 StuG. III armoured fighting vehicles in three companies instead of four. Since the detailed TOE was still not available, the reorganization process was far from being completed.

On 26 July at 1157 hours, the division put its troops on alert level I as a consequence of internal political developments in Italy (the dismissal of Mussolini and the formation of a new cabinet by General Badoglio). *Panzer-Abteilung 103* reported that it was in a state of readiness to march just 163 minutes after the alert had been ordered.

As a result of this event, the tone of local public opinion started to change from supporting the war to opposing it; in parallel with that, their attitude towards the German troops became decisively colder, sometimes even hostile. However, in the quartering area of *Panzer-Abteilung 103* in the area of San Lorenzo, citizens remained friendly with the Germans, who put that down to the firm control by fascists in the area. At the same time, the curfew imposed from 2100 hours on the Italian population was also extended to the German troops.[11]

On 27 July, all leave for the personnel was stopped until 8 August. Simultaneously, to be ready for any emergency, a liaison officer was sent from *Panzer-Abteilung 103* to the staff of *Oberbefehlshaber Süd* (Commander-in-Chief South) to facilitate communication.

On 29 July, however, alert level I was called off. On that day, the whole personnel of the unit were given instructions on the internal political situation in Italy. The soldiers' attention was specifically called to the importance of ignoring any insults from the Italian population.

On 1 August, *Panzer-Abteilung 103* had 42 StuG. III assault guns, three Panzer III command tanks[12] and two Panzer IB command tanks. All of them were combat-ready, except for an

10 *Kriegstagebuch der Panzer-Abteilung 103* (copy in author's possession), p. 10.

11 *Kriegstagebuch der Panzer-Abteilung 103* (copy in author's possession), p. 12.

12 One of them was equipped with a 5cm long-barrelled gun, the other two mounted 5 cm short-barrelled guns.

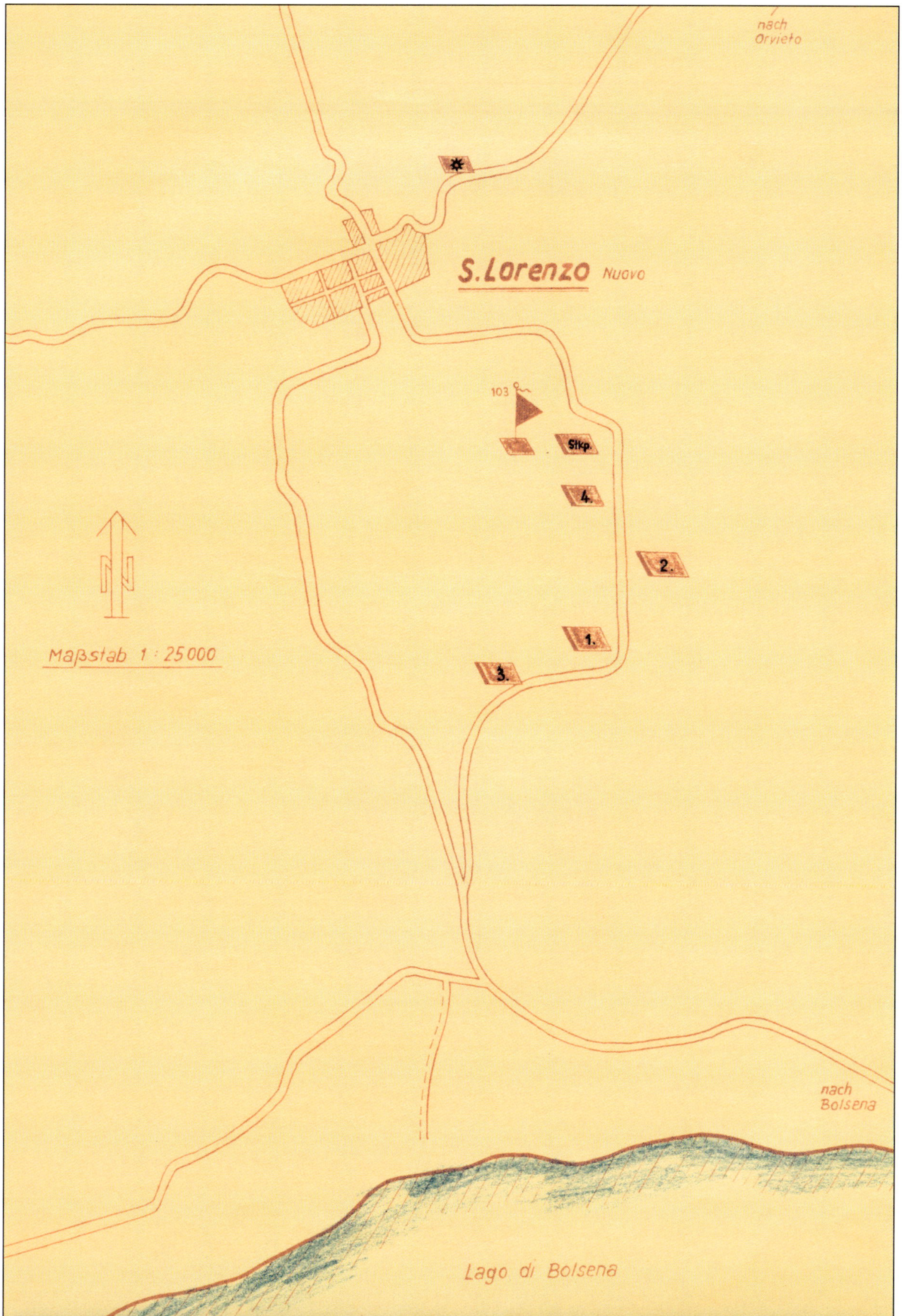

Quartering area of Panzer-Abteilung 103 on 25 July 1943

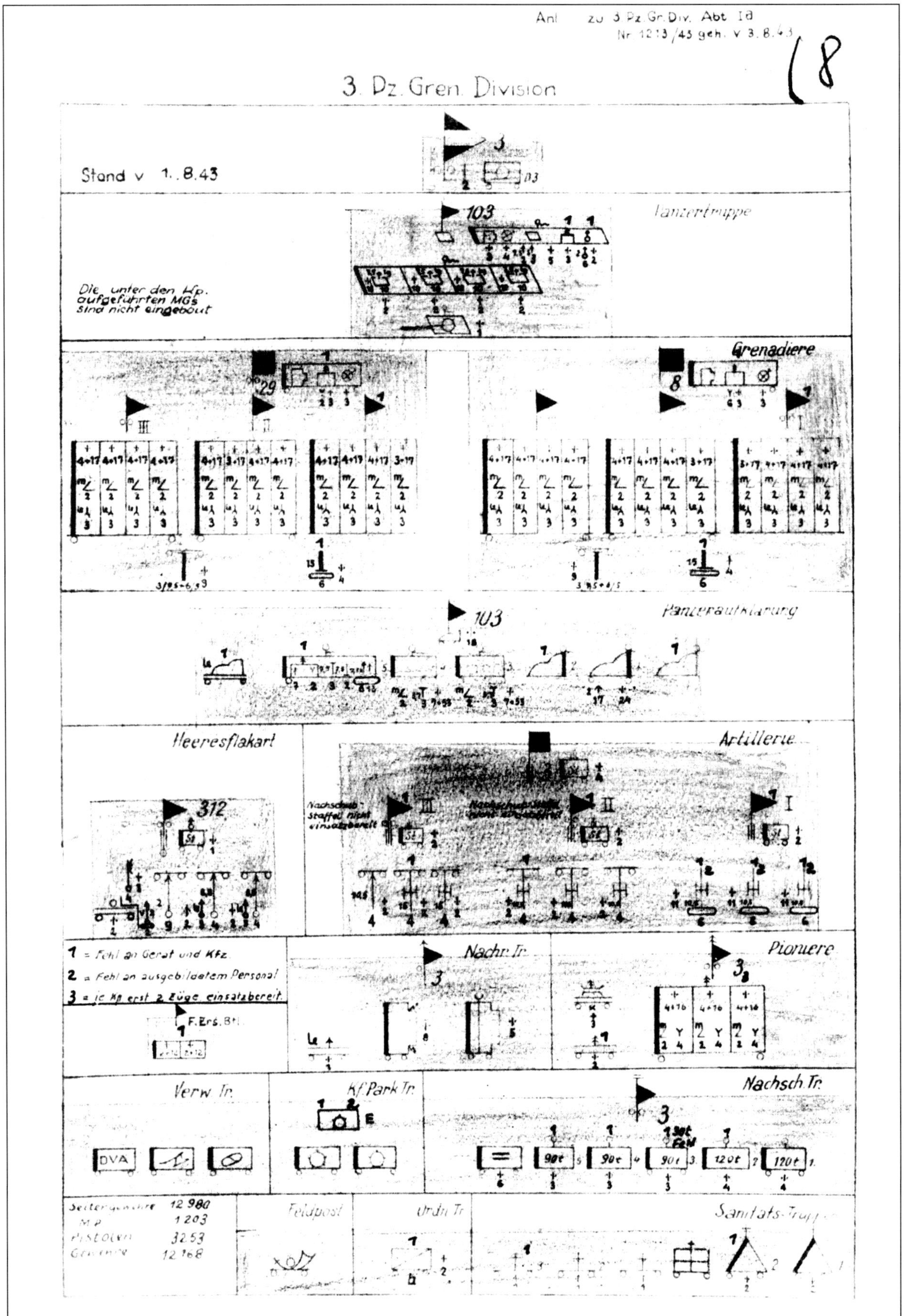

Order of battle of the 3. Panzergrenadier-Division on 1 August 1943

assault gun. According to the current TOE, *Panzer-Abteilung 103* should have possessed 93 Panzer IV and one Panzer III tanks, as well as two Panzer III command tanks; *Artillerie-Regiment (mot.) 3* should have had nine Panzer III AFVs.[13]

On the first days of August, due to the Allied landings on Sicily, *Panzer-Abteilung 103* was reinforced with additional armoured companies:

- **on 4 August,** the *4. Kompanie 'Fussgänger'* of *Panzer-Abteilung 215* arrived with 22 assault guns[14];
- **on 5 and 6 August,** 17 long-barrelled Panzer IV tanks (*Kompanie 'Paulus'*) from *Panzer-Regiment 26*[15], as well as 15 long-barrelled Panzer IV tanks (*Kompanie 'Fröde'*) of the *8./ Panzer-Regiment 'Hermann Göring'* were assigned to the unit.

Panzer-Abteilung 103 sent NCOs and enlisted men from its own personnel to the latter two companies as crews for the combat vehicles. Moreover, according to an order received at 0535 hours on 31 July, the Panzer IV tanks of *Panzer-Regiment 26* were fetched from Frosinone during a march carried out on tracks, and provided them with 340 shells plus machine-gun ammunition.[16]

On 8 August, *Oberleutnant* Fischer was subsequently promoted to the rank of *Hauptmann* as from 1 July 1943. On that day *Oberleutnant der Reserve* Willibald arrived at the unit to take up his assignment as engineer of *Panzer-Abteilung 103.*

On 10 August, the reorganization of the unit's order of battle was completed. Only three assault gun companies remained instead of the original four, so the 335 NCOs and enlisted men classified as supernumeraries were dispatched to the replacement unit on 13 and 14 August. At the same time *Oberleutnant* Wolter was transferred to *Panzer-Regiment 31, Oberleutnant* Bötticher and *Leutnant* Weidl were both assigned to the replacement unit.

On 11 August, the commander of *Panzer-Abteilung 103* issued an order about additional training requirements for the period between 16 August and 11 September. During these weeks, courses organized within the unit to provide further training for officers and NCOs were the focal point of activities. Attack manoeuvers and defensive tactics were heavily practiced by the soldiers during their tactical training. Continued efforts were made to maintain the physical fitness of the personnel.

On 20 August, *Panzer-Abteilung 103* conducted a command post exercise involving commanders of each unit of the *3. Panzergrenadier-Division* and even the division commander himself. In the course of the exercise, the basic principles of the employment of an armoured unit equipped with assault guns were laid down and the need for providing close support for the infantry was dealt with at length. One of the most significant principles instilled was that real effectiveness can be only achieved by concentrating forces and establishing focal points.

---

13 NARA T315, R173 (*3. Panzergrenadier-Division*), F000796.

14 The company was subordinated to *Panzer-Abteilung 103* at 1200 hours, on 1 August, 1943.

15 Soon, on 9 August, *Kompanie 'Paulus'* was switched from subordination to the unit to the control of *Kampfgruppe 'Büsing'* (a battle group of the *26. Panzer-Division*).

16 NARA T315, R173 (*3. Panzergrenadier-Division*), F000012, as well as F000803.

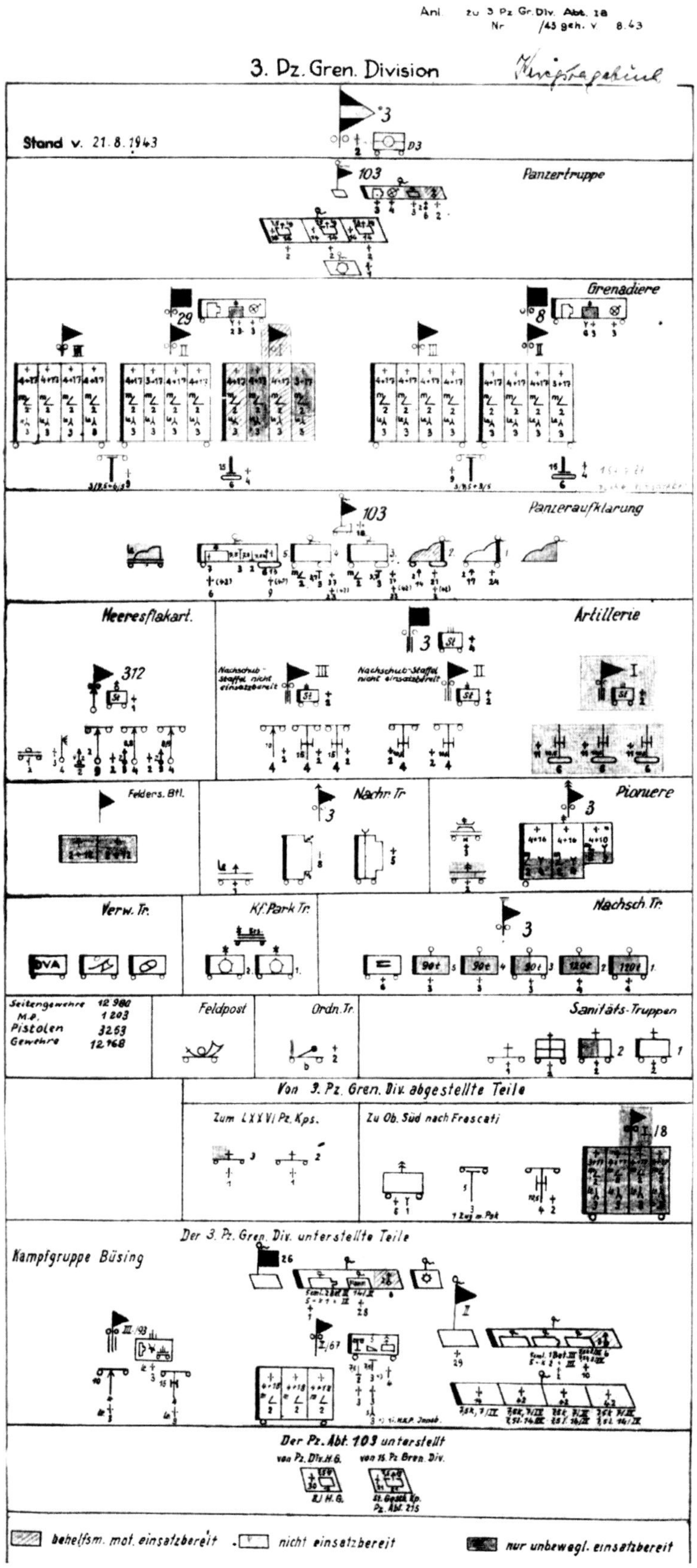

Order of battle of the 3. Panzergrenadier-Division on 21 August 1943

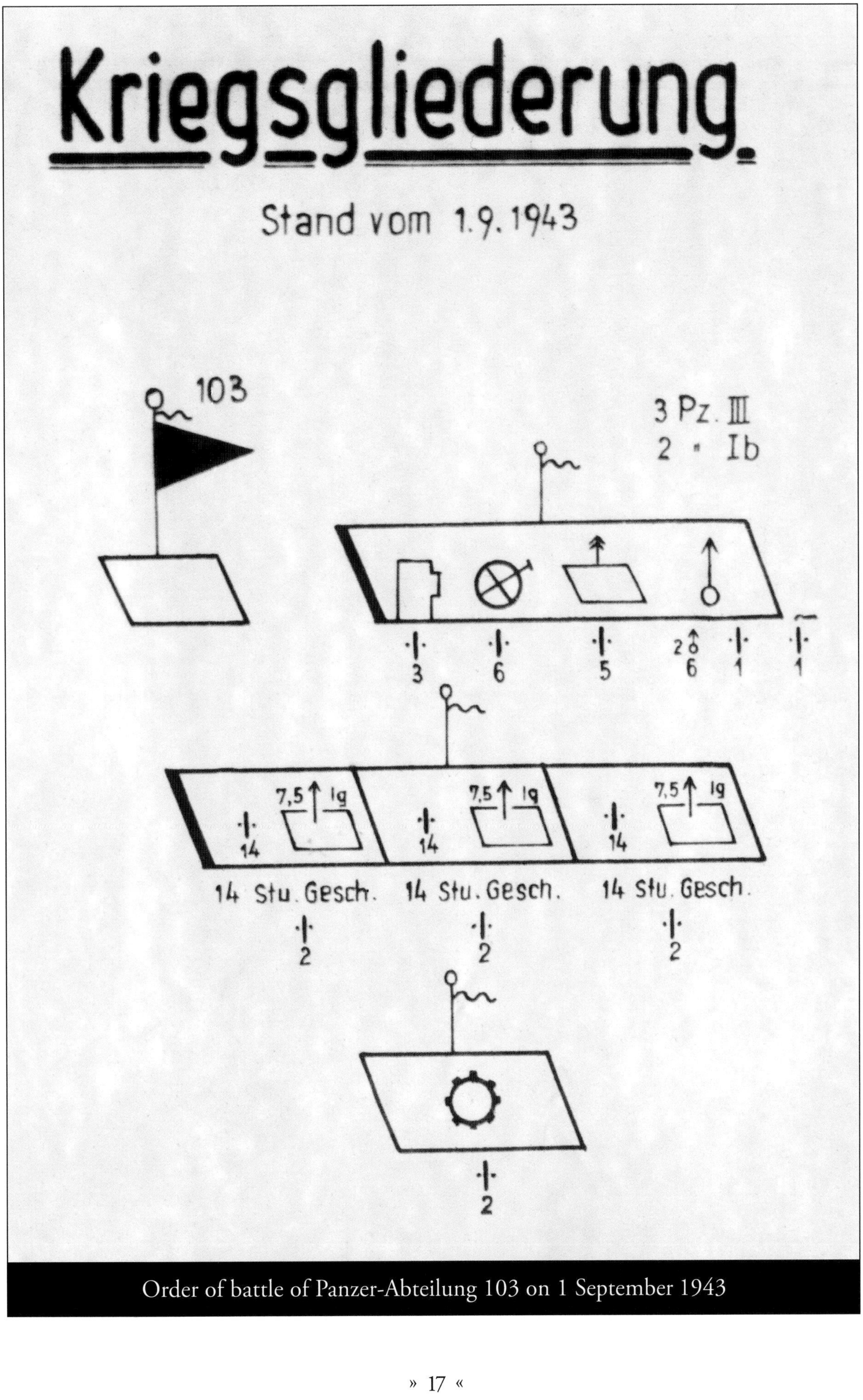

Order of battle of Panzer-Abteilung 103 on 1 September 1943

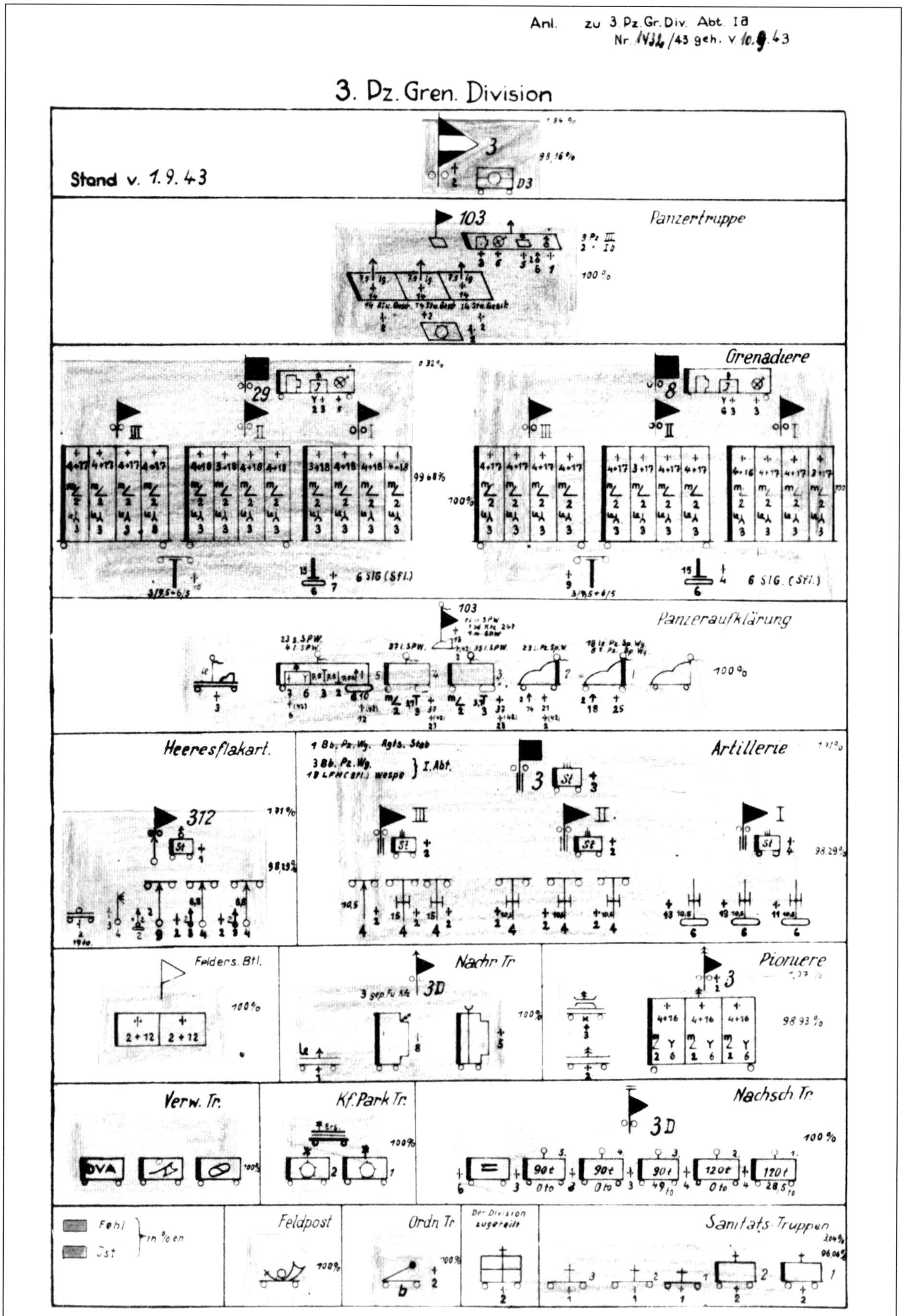

Order of battle of the 3. Panzergrenadier-Division on 1 September 1943

During August, the personnel of *Panzer-Abteilung 103* conducted training for soldiers belonging to the division's supply units in close combat against AFVs.

On 25 August, *Fahnenjunker Oberfeldwebel* Gräfe was transferred to the unit, and on the same day *Leutnant* Freiherr von Stosch-Debitsch was ordered to *Panzer-Erzatz und Ausbildungs-Abteilung 10,* the assigned replacement unit of the armoured *Abteilung.*

On 26 August, an additional 59 soldiers were transferred from *Panzer-Abteilung 103* to the replacement unit.[17]

On 29 August, orders were received from the division to organize a so-called 'motor week' *(Motor-Woche)* at *Panzer-Abteilung 103.* The purpose of this was to make the soldiers recognise the importance of maintenance and the proper handling of the vehicles. Different training courses were also conducted for e.g. fitters and drivers. Several inspections of motor vehicles were held during the week.

On 30 August the *Sturmgeschütz-Kompanie 'Fussgänger'* was detached from *Panzer-Abteilung 103* and dispatched to its parent unit, *15. Panzergrenadier-Division.*

On 1 September, according to the figures available, *Panzer-Abteilung 103* had 37 combat-ready StuG. III assault guns and three command combat vehicles. Another five assault guns were undergoing short-term repairs.[18]

On 2 September, armoured company *'Fröde'* was once again under the command of *Regiment 'Hermann Göring.'.*

On 5 September, the unit received orders from the division to be in readiness to march without delay at two hours' notice at the latest, having received the passwords 'Dora' and 'Martha.'

17 NARA T315, R173 (*3. Panzergrenadier-Division*), F000016.

18 NARA T315, R173 (*3. Panzergrenadier-Division*), F000732.

2

Italy pulls out of the war

On 8 September, at 1210 hours, *Panzer-Abteilung 103* was given notice by radio that it would soon receive the order for 'Martha' and therefore should keep its personnel together. *Hauptmann* Haen was summoned to the divisional command post to appear at 1400 hours. At 1650 hours the unit was informed by radio, that alarm codenamed 'Martha' had been ordered by 2000 hours.

Thus *Panzer-Abteilung 103* reached the state of readiness to march by 1930 hours. The commander of the unit issued orders to observe the British POW camp established in the area of Acquapendente without attracting too much attention so that prisoners wouldn't try to take any action, or attempt a mass escape, given the political events in Italy.

At 2350 hours the order to march was issued to march column 'A.' Contrary to previous orders, the *2. Kompanie* remained in subordination to the unit during the march.

On 9 September, at 0010 hours, following the receipt of orders, *Panzer-Abteilung 103* pulled into the division's march column immediately behind the command detachment in the following order: terrain reconnaissance platoon *(Erkundungszug),* advance command staff, a 2cm AA automatic cannon section, the combat echelons of the *1., 3.* and *2. Sturmgeschütz-Kompanien* with elements of the maintenance detachment; *Gefechtstroß I* (1st combat train), two 2cm AA automatic cannon sections, *Gefechtstroß II* (2nd combat train) plus a medical detachment. Having left their unit's area, the assigned route of march was: Montefiaskone–Viterbo–Vitralla–Oriolo and then, the newly assigned quartering area, Bracciano.

The unit passed through the settlement of Viterbo at around 0700 hours. At around 1000 hours, having left Oriolo, the lead elements of march column 'A' *(Marschgruppe 'Grosser')* encountered Italian resistance along the road. The lead company sustained minor losses. To outflank the resisting forces, the *1. Kompanie* of *Panzer-Abteilung 103* was brought forward and committed to action along the Oriolo–Canale road together with the *7. Kompanie* of *Grenadier-Regiment (mot.) 8.* No resistance was met afterwards and the two companies were able to advance at a good pace.[19]

19 *Kriegstagebuch der Panzer-Abteilung 103* (copy in author's possession), p. 20.

German attack towards Bracciano on 9 September 1943

Meanwhile *Bataillon 'Luckow'*[20] also resumed its march along the Oriolo–Manziana road without hindrance from the enemy. The commander of *Panzer-Abteilung 103, Hauptmann* Haen, joined the lead battalion. Manziana was taken without any resistance.

Having resumed their march toward Bracciano, the motorized infantry at the point of the advance reported an unexpected presence of Italian armour. The assaulting infantry were held up by violent defensive fire.

In response, *Hauptmann* Haen drew the *3. Kompanie* of *Panzer-Abteilung 103* forward to attack the enemy along the Manziana–Bracciano road and to its right, parallel to the German route of march. The *Sturmgeschütz-Kompanie* made a rapid progress but, because they were without the support of infantry, the company failed to penetrate Bracciano. To outflank the Italian fire, the company's assault gun platoon *'Heim'* was put into action to the left of the road. They made a bold dash forward but ran into an excellently concealed and camouflaged Italian position and came under heavy fire from AFVs as well as artillery. Three StuG. IIIs received hits and were disabled. Six of the StuG. crewmen were wounded.[21] In addition, the Germans lost two more knocked out AFVs, one AT gun, an infantry gun and also a heavy field howitzer. According to German evaluations, the resistance put up by the Italians was very smart: they launched a surprise attack from their skilfully concealed positions.[22]

At 1600 hours, as preparation for the next attack, the *2. Kompanie* was also brought forward. The two assault gun companies bypassed the settlement of Bracciano from the right before advancing on it without resistance. The defending Italian troops, having made preparations for the defence of the settlement at the eastern exit, started to withdraw. The infantry of the *3. Panzergrenadier-Division* and the *III. Bataillon* of *Grenadier-Regiment (mot.) 8* occupied Bracciano without suffering further losses.

After that, the infantry mounted the assault guns of the *2. Kompanie* and began moving out in hot pursuit of the retreating Italian troops. The mixed unit got to 12km south-east of Bracciano. At 1900 hours, orders came for the troops to halt and refresh themselves. The *2. Kompanie* took quarters in the area of Stazione della Crocicchie, while most of *Panzer-Abteilung 103* and the staff did likewise in the southern part of Bracciano.

At 2300 hours the unit's *1.* and *2. Sturmgeschütz-Kompanien* put under the command of *Bataillon 'Mollenhauer'*[23] by orders of the division. The battalion had been given the task of pursuing the retreating Italian forces and reaching the coast west of Rome.

This was because, at 1930 hours, the division had received orders from the superior *XI. Fliegerkorps* according to which *Panzer-Aufklärungs-Abteilung 103,* reinforced with the *II. Bataillon/ Grenadier-Regiment (mot.) 29,* two assault gun companies and a pioneer platoon were to reach Pratica di Mare via Ostia to link with the forces of the *2. Fallschirmjäger-Division.*[24] According to reports submitted during the evening, the Italian troops were ready to terminate their resistance. The Italian soldiers were to be disarmed and disbanded and the officers sent to POW camps.

20 The *III. Bataillon/Grenadier-Regiment (mot.) 8* under command of *Hauptmann* Luckow.

21 *Kriegstagebuch der Panzer-Abteilung 103* (copy in author's possession), p. 21.

22 NARA T315, R173 (*3. Panzergrenadier-Division*), F000021.

23 This was the *II. Bataillon* of *Grenadier-Regiment (mot.) 29.*

24 NARA T315, R173 (*3. Panzergrenadier-Division*), F000022.

On 10 September, in the morning, *Marschgruppe 'Grosser'* set out again. *Panzer-Abteilung 103* pulled into the marching column at 1045 hours. However, having reached Pte. Piconcella, its advance was halted, due to the fact, that negotiations with the divisions were still ongoing. *Panzer-Abteilung 103* encamped along the road in a barren stubble-field, where they remained until the next evening. During their short rest, the unit performed maintenance and took stock of captured equipment.

In the evening the unit was informed that the *1.* and *2. Sturmgeschütz-Kompanien*, subordinated to the *II. Bataillon* of *Grenadier-Regiment (mot.) 29,* were brought forward to the front line in the area of Naples. Thus, besides the supply subunits, only the *3. Sturmgeschütz-Kompanie* remained subordinated to the staff of *Panzer-Abteilung 103.* By means of a motorcycle courier, the unit's workshop, which had been located in the area of San Lorenzo from 8 September, was ordered to Bracciano where it settled in the local Italian garrison for armoured troops.

According to the formal history of the *3. Panzergrenadier-Division,* the two assault gun companies of *Panzer-Abteilung 103* linked up with the forces of the *2. Fallschirmjäger-Division* on this day in Rome.[25] However, this is not mentioned in the unit's own war diary.

On 11 September, at 1730 hours, the staff of *Panzer-Abteilung 103* received orders to take over and secure the coastal area. An hour later the unit pulled into the marching column of *Marschgruppe 'Grosser'* again. They bypassed the Italian capital from a westerly direction. The German vehicles encountered several roadblocks in the area of Rome, significantly slowing their advance. Due to that, the armoured unit reached its new quartering area only at dawn next day.

On 12 September at 0330 hours, *Panzer-Abteilung 103* reached the town of Aprilia. At the same time *Panzer-Abteilung 103* was placed in the divisional reserve.

The unit's command post was established in a manor 2km north of Aprilia. The *3. Sturmgeschütz-Kompanie* remained inside the town. The supply columns quartered immediately east of the battalion command post.

At night orders were received by radio, according to which *Hauptmann* Haen should lend a hand in disarming the Italian divisions located in Rome and in collecting their equipment.

The handover of the Italian weapons began at 1000 hours at the northern bridge of the River Tiber. On behalf of the Germans *Generalleutnant* Gräser and *Hauptmann* Haen and his adjutant were present and also elements of an infantry company. As for the Italians, it was the commanders of the *12. 'Sassari'* and the *13. 'Re'* infantry divisions that participated in the negotiations. Both parties agreed that the Italian troops would hand over their weapons and vehicles at a specific place. However, it soon became clear, that the German detachment – small in number – was unable to carry out the takeover. As a result, *Generalmajor* Seibt[26] was assigned to that task from then on, and *Hauptmann* Haen returned to the command post of *Panzer-Abteilung 103.*

25 *See* Dieckhoff, Gerhard: *3. Infanterie-Division – 3. Infanterie-Division (mot.) – 3. Panzergrenadier-Division* Cuxhaven, s.a., p. 249.

26 *Generalmajor* Conrad Seibt served as general on special duty with *Oberbefehlshaber Süd* at that time.

Similarly, the largest proportion of the work to be done was to take over and check the Italian war material in the area of Aprilia. By orders of the division the unit had to inspect each and every Italian tank and assault gun and, if they were combat-ready, to integrate them into the plan-of-fire of the coastal defence. Simultaneously, conditions for a probable German armoured counterattack were to be considered, should the Allied troops land in the area.

In the afternoon, the *3. Sturmgeschütz-Kompanie* of the unit marched into Anzio as a demonstration of power to reinforce the authority of the German infantry securing the area of Anzio and Nettuno. In the evening *Panzer-Abteilung 103* was put under command of the *9. Kompanie* of *Grenadier-Regiment (mot.) 8,* which secured the coast in the area of Cerveteri.

During the next two days, captured Italian war material was sorted out and maintenance was performed. The staff was yet to receive any information about the unit's *1. and 2. Sturmgeschütz-Kompanien.*

On 13 September, *Panzer-Abteilung 103* was ordered to send supernumerary soldiers and drivers of armoured units to Frascati where they would take over captured Italian AFVs and vehicles.[27]

On 15 September, looting and retaining captured Italian vehicles were strictly forbidden according to an order issued by the unit's commander.

27 NARA T315, R173 (*3. Panzergrenadier-Division*), F000025. According to figures for 17 September 1943, the division captured 14 combat-ready tanks (including seven Italian-made ones) plus two operational assault guns, and another 15 AFVs in repair workshops. *See* NARA T315, R173 (*3. Panzergrenadier-Division*), F001146. From the Italian troops, armoured division 'Centauro', concentrated in the area of Rome, also possessed German AFVs.

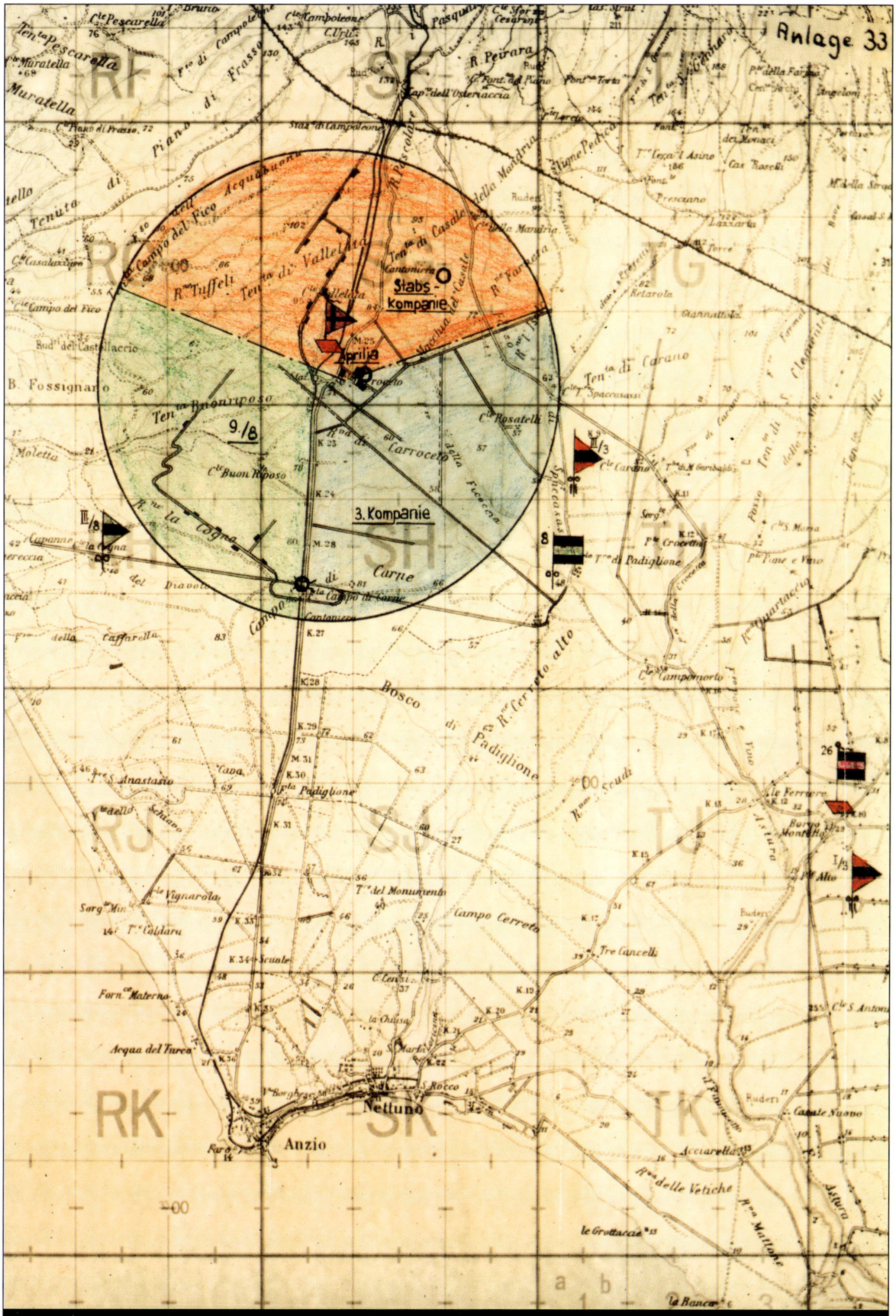

Situation map, 13 September 1943

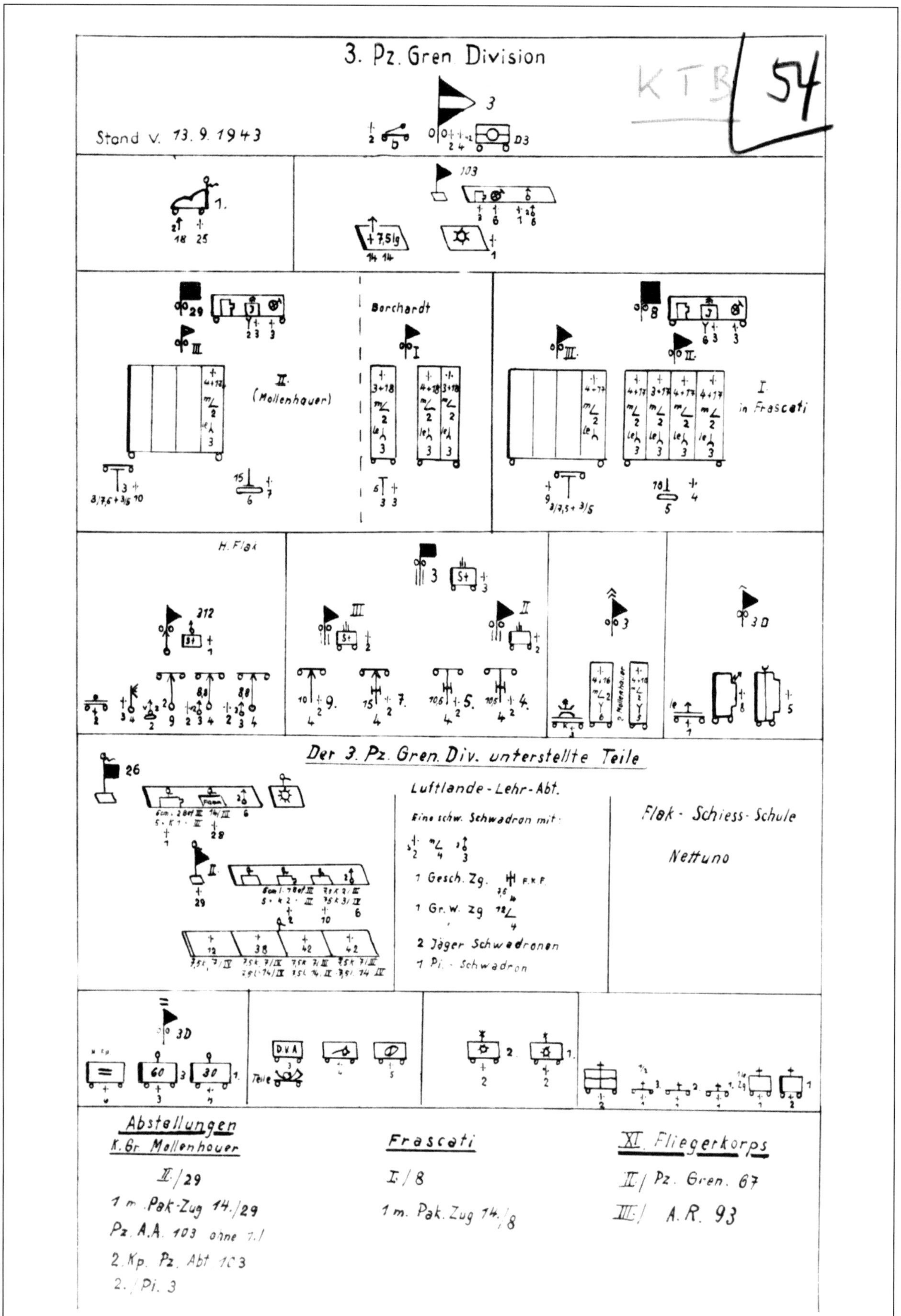

Order of battle of the 3. Panzergrenadier-Division on 13 September 1943

3

Fighting from Salerno to the River Volturno

Afterwards, *Panzer-Abteilung 103* prepared for all round defence in the area of Aprilia. The *3. Sturmgeschütz-Kompanie* built covers for their StuG. III assault guns 2km west and south-west of the town. The staff company established infantry positions south and south-east of Aprilia.

On 17 September *Oberleutnant der Reserve* Willi Hinzpeter arrived at the staff with new information about the *1. Sturmgeschütz-Kompanie* that had been sent into action on the Salerno front line. The company had been withdrawn from combat – except for the assault gun platoon *'Gran'* – and was put under the command of *Panzer-Abteilung 103* again. *Leutnant* Gran described the company's withdrawal from combat in his dispatch:

'[...]

During the night from the 9th to the 10th of September, the battle group of Oberstleutnant *Mollenhauer with the 2. Kompanie (commander:* Hauptmann *Heller) and the 1. Kompanie (commander:* Leutnant *Gran) of* Panzer-Abteilung 103 *attached to them, were pulled out from the south-western part of Bracciano. On the same night we came round Rome from an easterly direction, and reached the area 20km south of Rome before noon on the 10th of September. We were given the task of supporting the* [2.] Fallschirmjäger-Division *south of Rome. In the afternoon we received orders to resume our march to the* XIV. Panzerkorps *north of Naples. During our march there, both armoured companies had been detached from battle group 'Mollenhauer' by orders of general Student[28], and we were supposed to have provided support for the paratroopers in eliminating the last traces of the resistance put up by the Italians south of Rome. However, the attack was called off due to the fact that Rome had surrendered by then.*

Therefore we followed battle group 'Mollenhauer' *by another night march along Highway 6, and on the 11th of September we reached the northern area of Aversa. Thus, connection was restored between Rome and Naples without a single shot from our side.*

28 *General der Fallschirmtruppe* Karl Student was the commander of the *XI. Fliegerkorps* at that time.

In Naples itself, there was unrest caused by troops loyal to Badoglio, communist gangs and looting civilians. Because of that, on the 12th of September, battle group 'Mollenhauer', *with the support of a platoon of the* 2. Kompanie *of* Panzer-Abteilung 103, *was ordered to advance to the port of Naples to restore public order. Within the sea of houses, armoured support proved to be clumsy, and only a few shots thundered in the air.*

We received orders as early as next day (the 13th of September) at noon to resume our march towards the Salerno front line, and on the night from the 13th to the 14th of September, we reached our readiness position at Sanseverino (10km north of Salerno). During this march we were struck by low-level ground attacks carried out by American fighters for the first time, although they proved to be unsuccessful. Sanseverino was air bombed all through the night, causing severe damage only to buildings.

[...]

On the 14th of September both armoured [StuG.] companies were pulled out of battle group 'Mollenhauer' *and put under the battle group commanded by* Oberst *Schmalz* (Division 'Hermann Göring'). *We were given the task to make rapid progress westwards on the Ogliora–San Mango–Pazzano road via Ponte Fratte (3km north of Salerno), then move out southwards to Pontecarno via Filetta. At noon* Panzer-Regiment 'Hermann Göring' *took the lead, followed by us with our assault guns. The weak resistance put up by enemy AT guns and reconnaissance armoured cars between San Mango and Pezzano was eliminated by the lead AFV-s. By the evening the attack had got to the area 3km south of Filetta, where stiff resistance was encountered. Due to that, further attack was postponed until the 15th of September.*

The terrain, quite mountainous there, caused extreme difficulties, and because of that, the armoured combat vehicles could hardly leave the highway. So we had to provide fire support with the assault guns from the San Mango–Pezzano road on the immense vine-growing area towards the south up to 2 or 3km. With our AFVs confined to the road, the enemy's naval artillery had the chance to operate more efficiently. The cruisers anchored in the Salerno Bay mainly kept the road between Ponte Fratte and San Mango under heavy fire directed by observation balloons.

In the evening, we established a covering position eastwards and were under constant heavy artillery fire resulting in losing two wounded in my company. I ordered a platoon under command of Leutnant *Gehlen to the Molinetto Bridge (1km east-south-east of Filetta) to secure it, especially against a surprise attack. These assault guns had no grenadier support whatsoever and were totally left to their own resources since there was a deep ravine between them and the company. Communication could only be maintained on foot and by radio. The platoon was attacked by British reconnaissance patrols, but they were repelled, partly with machine guns dismounted* [from assault guns].

On the 15th of September, in the afternoon, Panzer-Regiment 'Hermann Göring' *resumed its attack towards Pontecagno. Having reached its objective, the assault guns were to secure the settlement while the armoured combat vehicles linked up with the* 16. Panzer-Division *eastwards at Battibaglia. We provided cover with all the assault guns for the attack towards south-east, operating as artillery from a hill. However the attack ground to a halt because, on the highway – and this proved to be extremely serpentine – 3km south of Filetta, only three armoured fighting vehicles at most could be deployed from the whole regiment and they were stopped in their tracks by enemy AT-*

guns. The first three combat vehicles were knocked out by the enemy employing a new tactic: they set up the AT guns heavily camouflaged to the left and right of the road, let the armoured fighting vehicles approach to within 40m at a bend in the road then, having fired one or two rounds, the crews of the AT guns fled headlong to nowhere, leaving all their equipment behind.

[...]

On the 15th of September orders were received to break contact with the enemy and take up positions 6 or 7km south of Salerno. This was carried out in the following way: an assault gun platoon entered each settlement to secure it while the road was cleared of troops and equipment up to the following point to be secured.

The evacuation lasted quite a while, because several AFVs had to be towed away. The securing assault guns – with only insignificant support of grenadiers or completely without it – were constantly having trouble with enemy reconnaissance patrols. The enemy had so far ventured ahead on the road only with armoured cars of which we knocked out five. Subsequently we got into trouble with the enemy artillery as well, since the British cruisers provided violent fire support. On the night from the 20th to the 21st of September we reached the new front line of the infantry at Coperschia–Cologna following the Pezzano–San Cipriano–San Mango–Ogliara–Ponte Fratte–Capezzano road. An assault gun platoon remained there with securing tasks, the rest of the unit marched off 6km to the north, to Fisciano, to have a rest.

During the following days, the enemy occupied the hills on two sides of Coperschia–Cologna with significant infantry forces, and by so doing, they pushed back our front line to Baronissi by the 25th of September. On the 27th of September 1943, we were relieved from assignment with Division 'Hermann Göring' *and began our march back to* Panzer-Abteilung 103, *which we reached on the 29th of September at Cervaro (south of Cassino).*[29]'

On 18 September, *Leutnant* Schwäpenheuer assumed duties as adjutant of the unit. From then on, *Leutnant* Kock fulfilled the duties of the orderly officer.

On 22 September, the division reported to the superior *XIV. Panzerkorps* that its only reserve available was battle group '*Büsing*', made up of the staff and a *Sturmgeschütz-Kompanie* of *Panzer-Abteilung 103* and the *I. Bataillon* of *Grenadier-Regiment (mot.) 29.*[30]

On 25 September, *Panzer-Abteilung 103* received orders to march from the area of Aprilia towards Mignano at 0600 hours. The unit was led by *Hauptmann* Fischer, the commander of the *3. Kompanie*, in the following order:

- staff,
- *3. Kompanie*,
- elements of the *1. Kompanie*
- 1st combat train (*Gefechtstroß I*),
- 2nd combat train (*Gefechtstroß II*).

29 *Kriegstagebuch der Panzer-Abteilung 103* (copy in author's possession), pp. 28-31.
30 NARA T315, R173 (*3. Panzergrenadier-Division*), F000029.

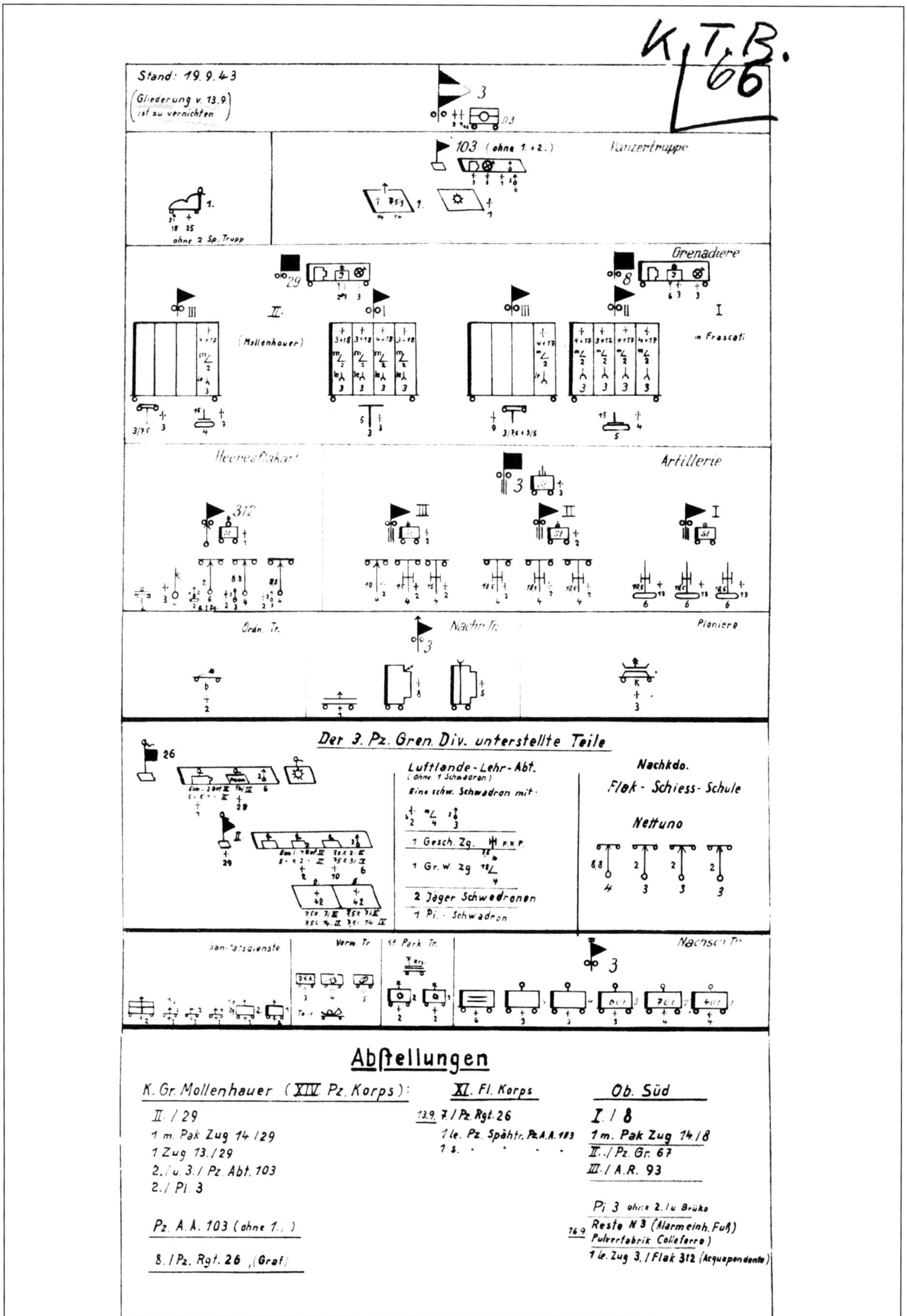

Order of battle of the 3. Panzergrenadier-Division on 19 September 1943

The discipline of the marching troops was excellent by this time. Nothing disturbed their progress until they reached the area of Arce, where the unit was attacked from behind by six American fighters operating at low altitude. The *Gefechtstroß II* column – the tail of the march column – suffered the heaviest losses. Two vehicles had to be written off as total losses: the office truck of the *1. Kompanie* and one of the trailers of the staff company that was transporting fuel. Both vehicles were completely burnt out. The AA automatic cannon platoon lost two wounded. Due to the enemy's significant air superiority, the unit was able to take up its assigned quartering area in Cervaro only after nightfall.

On 28 September, a German station command *(Ortskommandantur)* was established with *Hauptmann* Haen as its commander. The actual tasks were carried out by the commander of the terrain reconnaissance platoon, *Leutnant* Beschnidt.

On the same day, during a meeting, the *3. Panzergrenadier-Division* made a request to the representative of the chief inspector of the armoured troops to re-equip *Panzer-Abteilung 103* with tanks instead of assault guns.[31]

On 29 September, in the afternoon, the *1.* and *2. Kompanien* arrived; both had fought at Salerno before under command of *Panzer-Division 'Hermann Göring'.*

Before noon, *Panzer-Abteilung 103* received orders to hold themselves in readiness to march. According to these plans they were supposed to start off at noon. However these orders were retracted the following day.

On 30 September, *Oberfeldwebel* Fischer and *Fahnenjunker-Unteroffiziere* Zimmermann, Fritsche and Luft were sent to *Panzer-Ersatz- und Ausbildungs-Abteilung 10* in Zinten to attend a course there.

On 1 October, *Oberleutnant der Reserve* Hinzpeter and *Leutnant* Geisser were ordered to the division to set up a terrain reconnaissance staff there.

On 2 October, in the morning, *Hauptmann* Haen drove to *Grenadier-Regiment (mot.) 29* to a meeting. On his return, his unit received orders at 1025 hours to carry out a march southwards. The designated march route was as follows: Cervaro–Mignano–Baia é Latina–Dragoni.

On 3 October, in the early hours, the staff of the unit took up its quarters in San Marco, the *1. Kompanie* in Piana di Caiazzo, the *2. Kompanie* company in Ruviano, the *3. Kompanie* in Castel Campagnano and the *Gefechtstroß I* and *II* columns in Alvignano.

The *1.* and *2. Kompanien* were sent into combat with their assault guns on the front line along the River Volturno. The *2. Kompanie* was still held in the reserve of *Panzer-Abteilung 103.*

On 5 October, the staff of the unit was sent to the command post of battle group *'Moeller'* in the area of Ortensia. In the afternoon the unit gave assistance in transporting the Italian civilian population, since the area behind the front line had to be evacuated. Italian men between the age of 15 and 60 were called up for labour service. According to records taken at 1900 hours, the *1. Kompanie* of *Panzer-Abteilung 103* was still located at Piana di Caiazza,

31 NARA T315, R173 (*3. Panzergrenadier-Division*), F000032.

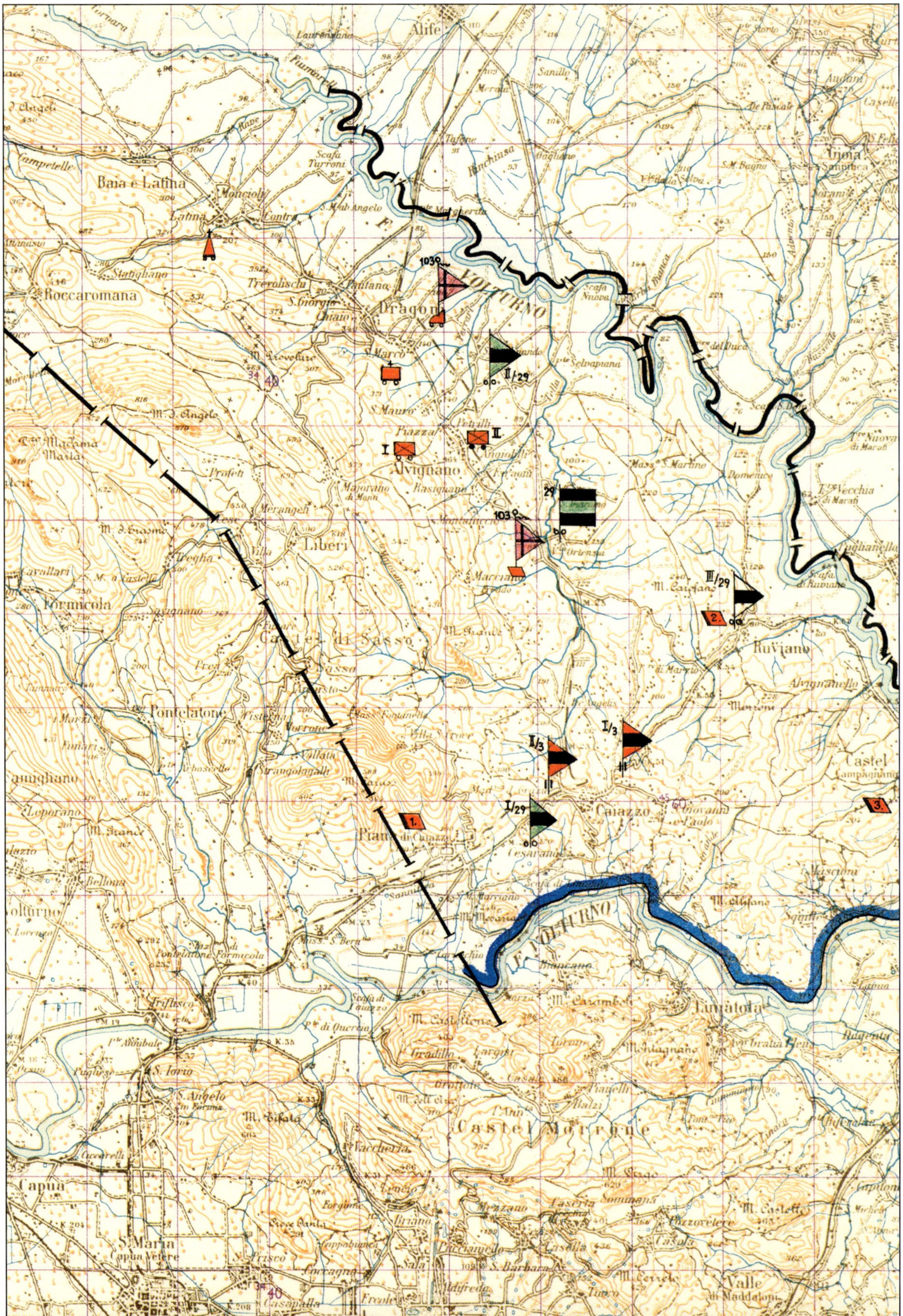

Quartering area of Panzer-Abteilung 103 on 3 October 1943

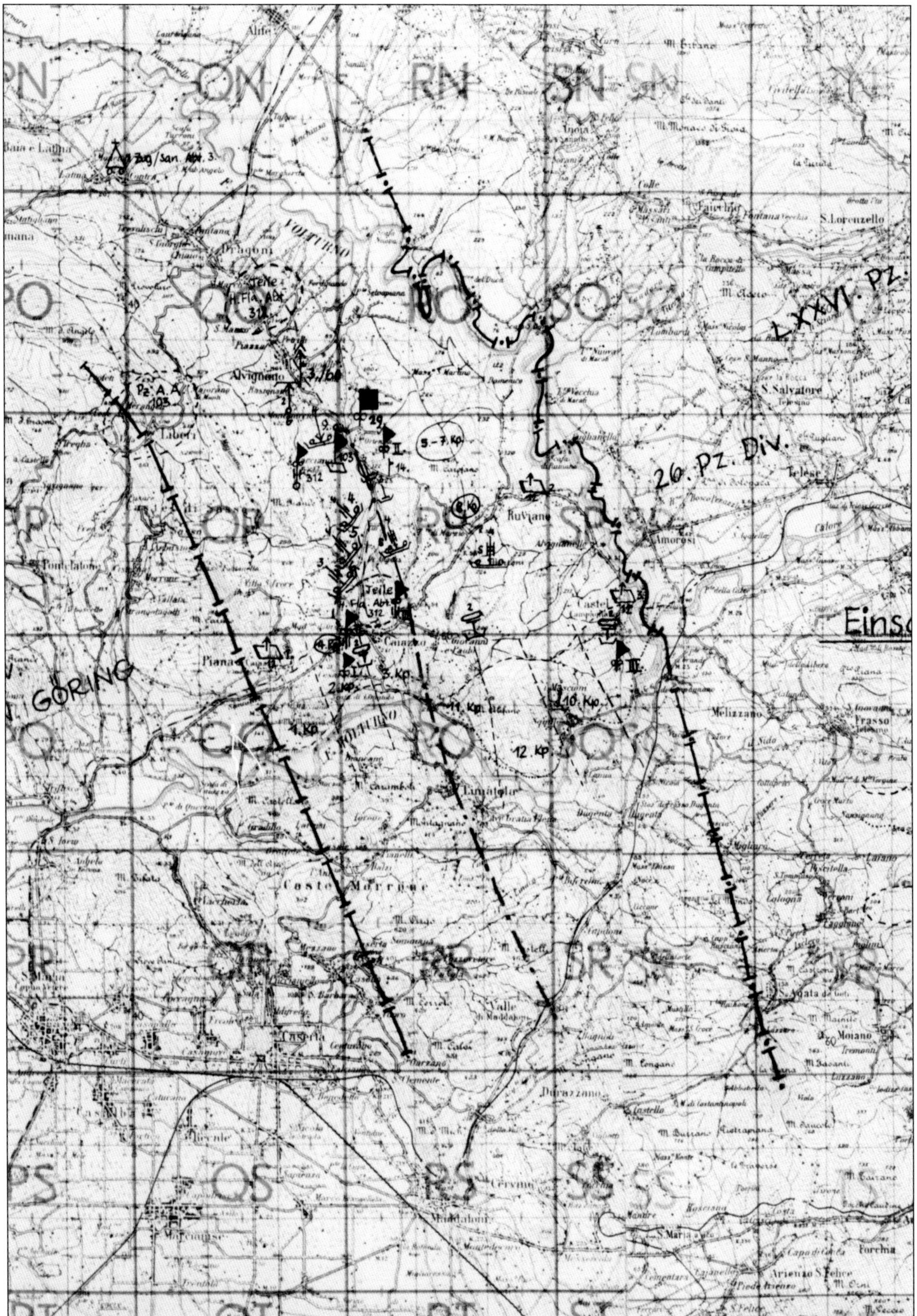

Situation map, 5 October 1943

the *2. Kompanie* was stationed at Ruviano and the *3. Kompanie* at Castel Campagnano, each company with 12 combat-ready assault guns at their disposal.[32]

On the night from 5 to 6 October, a report arrived from the *3. Kompanie* according to which the assault gun platoon *'Geisser'*, ordered to the area of Dugenta together with subordinated grenadiers and pioneers as an advance guard, was under increasing enemy pressure.

On 7 October, *Hauptmann* Haen received orders from *Oberst* Moeller[33] to take over command of the defence zone of *Panzer-Aufklärungs-Abteilung 26* (a unit belonging to the *26. Panzer-Division*). By so doing, *Panzer-Aufklärungs-Abteilung 103,* as well as the *5. Kompanie* of *Grenadier-Regiment (mot.) 29,* came under the command of *Panzer-Abteilung 103*. The *I. Abteilung* of *Artillerie-Regiment (mot.) 3* with 18 Wespe 10.5mm self-propelled howitzers and elements of *Nebelwerfer-Regiment 71* also operated in this sector.[34]

Having reconnoitred the area thoroughly, *Hauptmann* Haen arrived back at his unit command post at around 1600 hours. The unit started on its march towards its new positions after nightfall. *Panzer-Abteilung 103's* command post was set up at Ceze C. Manno.

On 9 October, during the noon hours, there were 12 combat-ready StuG. III assault guns in each of the three companies of *Panzer-Abteilung 103,* subordinated to battle group *'Moeller'*. The *1. Kompanie* was situated between Telese and San Salvatore, the *3. Kompanie* along the San Salvatore–Amorosi highway and the *2. Kompanie* was located 4km west-north-west of Amorosi.[35]

On 10 October, the new staff surgeon, Dr Mayer, arrived at the unit. In the afternoon, the division commander, *Generalleutnant* Gräser, and *Hauptmann* Haen made their round of inspection in the defensive positions along the River Volturno. At that time only three battalions of *Grenadier-Regiment (mot.) 29,* two artillery battalions of *Artillerie-Regiment (mot.) 3, Panzer-Aufklärungs-Abteilung 103* and the assault guns of *Panzer-Abteilung 103* were fighting on the 20km-wide front line.[36]

On 11 October, from 0900 hours the Allied artillery had shelled the German positions for six hours, then at 1530 hours an attack was launched, but was repelled by the forces of *Panzer-Abteilung 103's* battle group.[37] German reconnaissance identified the forces of the US 34th Infantry Division in that sector and also established the fact that part of the Italian civilian population joined the fighting to support the Allied troops.

Panzer-Abteilung 103 had 38 combat-ready StuG. III assault guns and three command tanks on that day.[38]

On 12 October, Allied artillery fire was poured upon Telese for three hours. The settlement, as well as Colle Cagliano fell into the hands of troops of the US 45th Infantry Division twice, but was taken back by the *I. Bataillon* of *Grenadier-Regiment (mot.)* 8 with the support of the

32 NARA T315, R173 (*3. Panzergrenadier-Division*), F000573.
33 He was the commander of *Grenadier-Regiment (mot.) 29.*
34 Dieckhoff, Gerhard: *3. Infanterie-Division – 3. Infanterie-Division (mot.) – 3. Panzergrenadier-Division* Cuxhaven, s.a., p. 253.
35 NARA T315, R173 (*3. Panzergrenadier-Division*), F000562.
36 NARA T315, R173 (*3. Panzergrenadier-Division*), F000038.
37 NARA T315, R173 (*3. Panzergrenadier-Division*), F000544.
38 NARA T315, R173 (*3. Panzergrenadier-Division*), F000545.

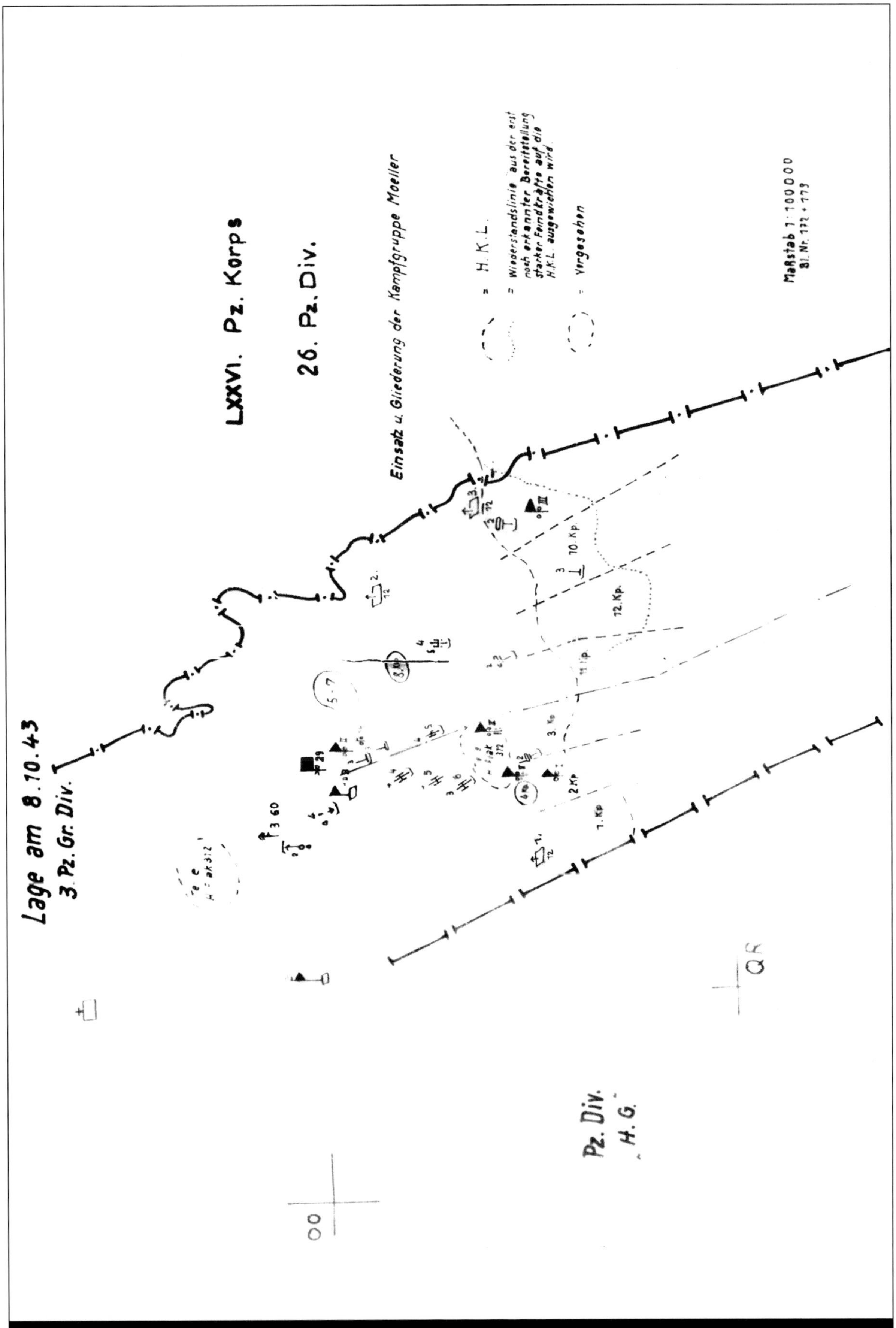

Situation map, 8 October 1943

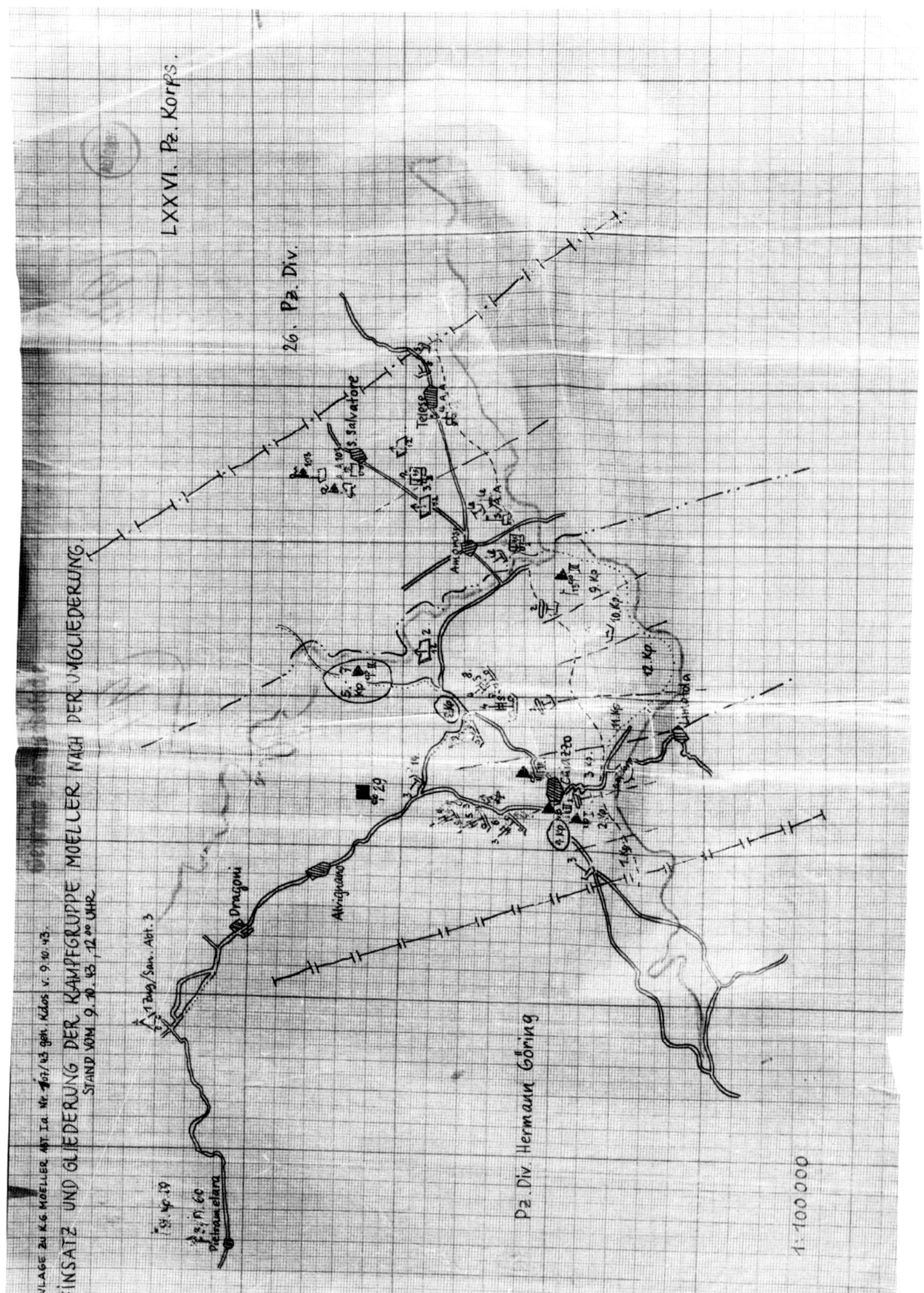

Situation map, 9 October 1943

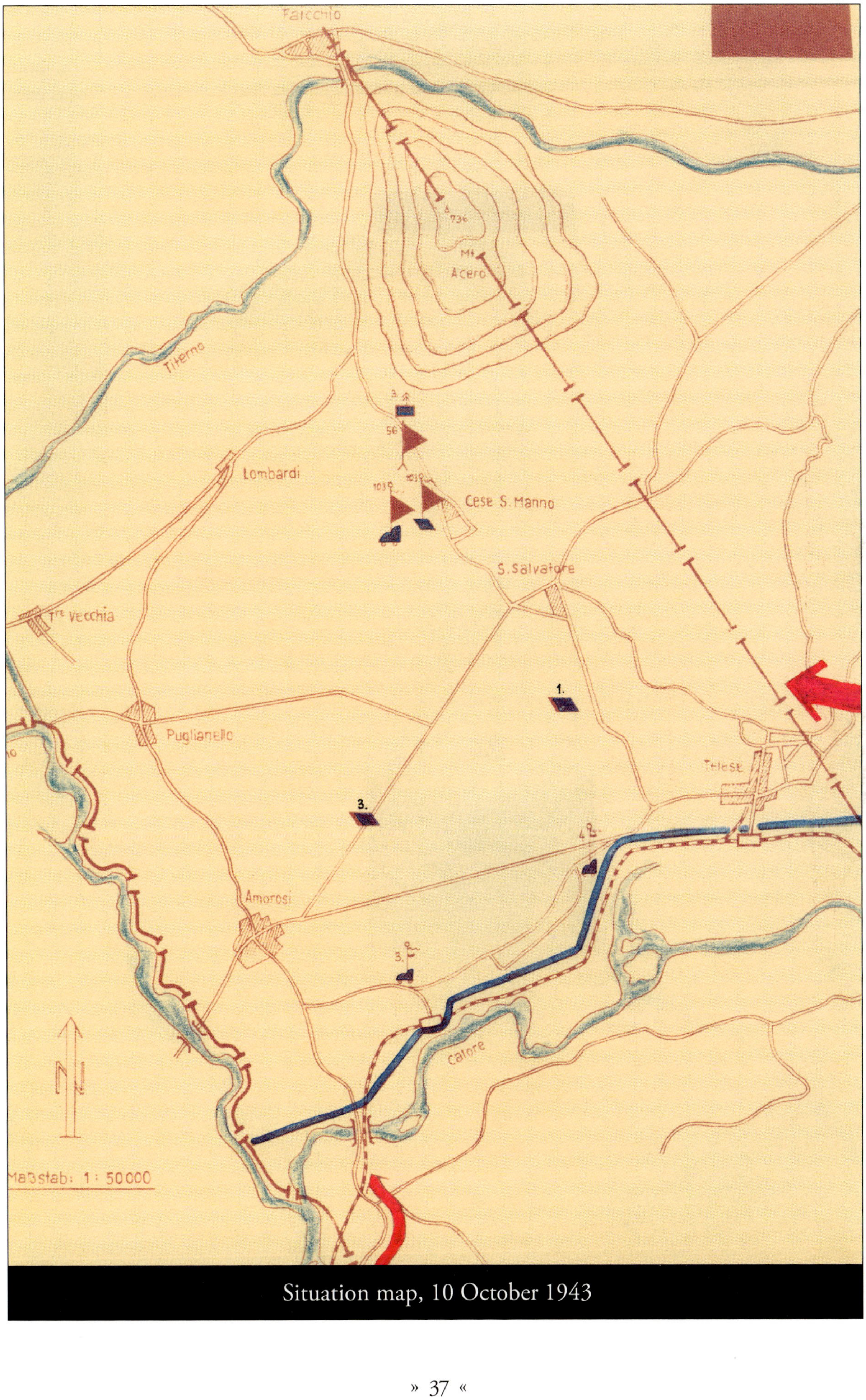

Situation map, 10 October 1943

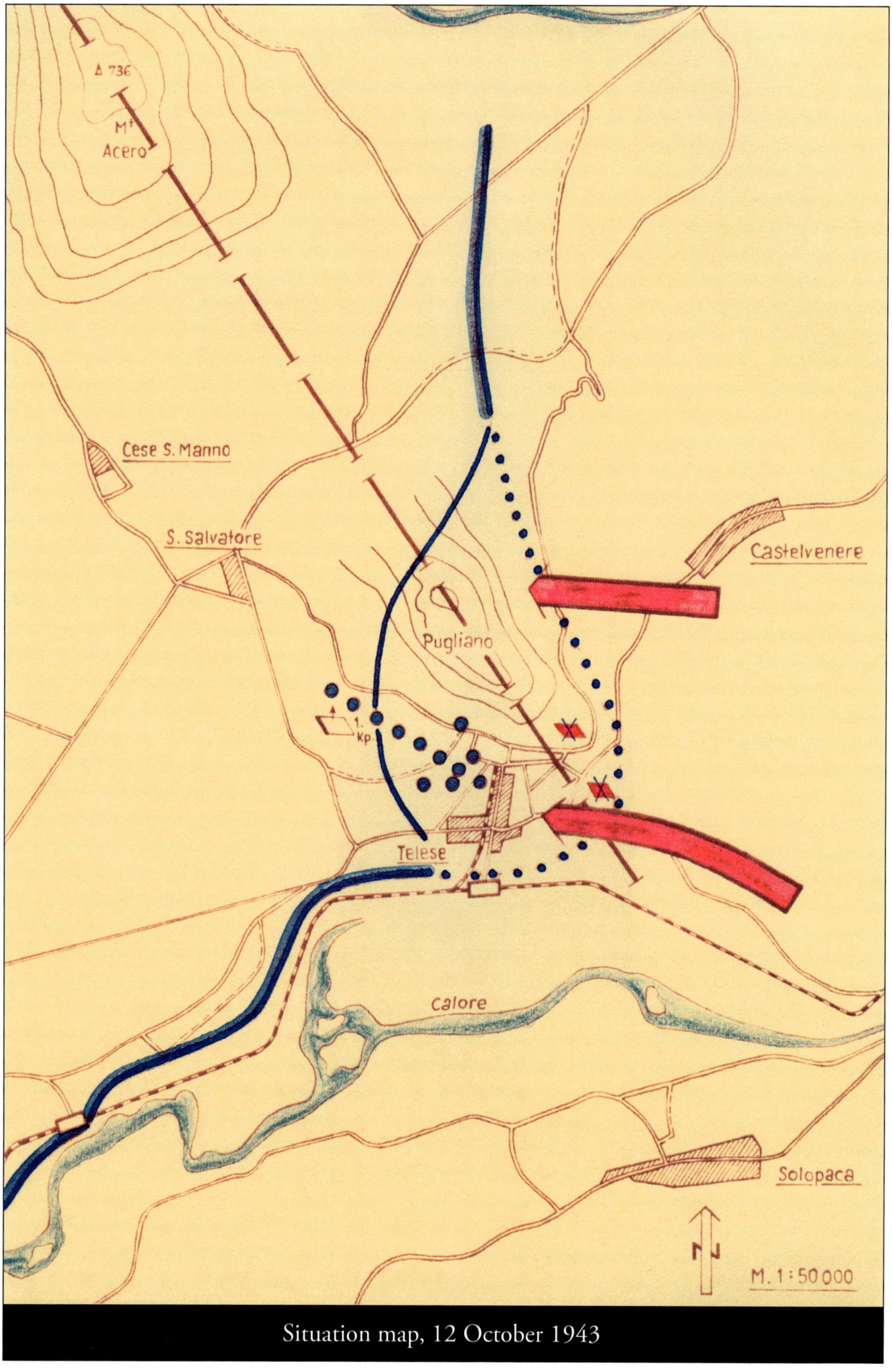

Situation map, 12 October 1943

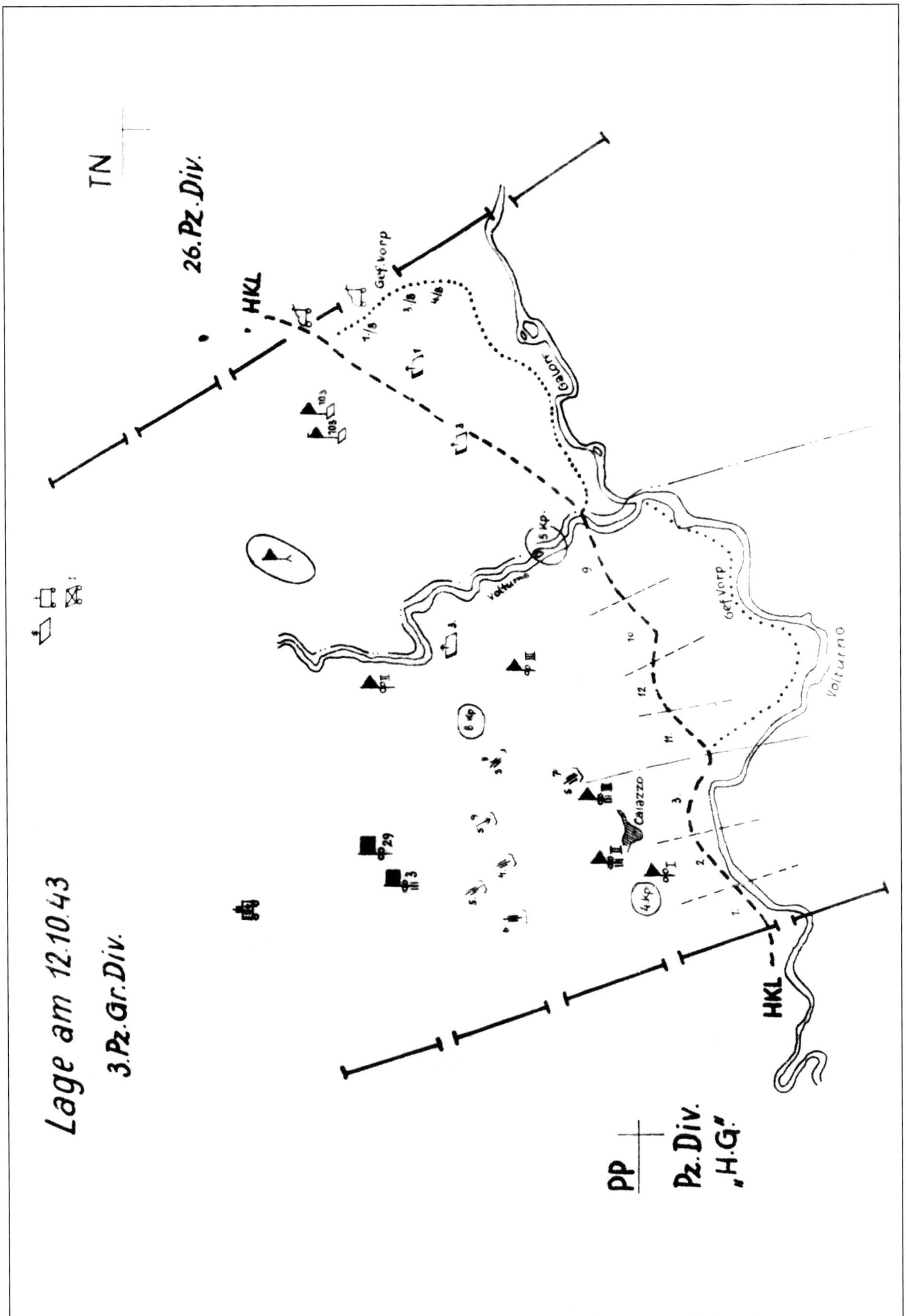

Situation map, 12 October 1943

assault guns of *Panzer-Abteilung 103*, carrying out counterthrusts both times.[39] During the fighting the *1. Kompanie* knocked out two Allied AFVs.[40] Although the German troops suffered heavy losses (e.g. the *3. Kompanie* of *Grenadier-Regiment (mot.) 8* lost 75% of its strength), they held their positions. In the end, however, the weakened troops were ordered to retreat to the so-called 'Friedrich' line to perform a delaying action and by so doing gave up the defence of Telese. The German rear guard detachments were all supported by assault guns.[41]

One of the assault gun platoons of *Panzer-Abteilung 103* supported battle group *'Viebig'* of the *26. Panzer-Division* which halted the elements of the US 45th Infantry Division in the area of Fontana and south-east of Acero. On the other hand, the Americans occupied San Salvatore and the hills north of the settlement.[42]

On 13 October, *Panzer-Abteilung 103* retreated in the midst of sporadic Allied artillery harassing fire with enemy reconnaissance detachments operating against them. Minor attacks launched on Telese and on the hills to the north were repelled three times by the Germans and counted 35-40 dead Americans in front of their defensive positions.[43]

On 14 October, at 0530 hours, fierce artillery fire was poured onto the area of Fontana and Faicchio, along the River Titerno. The Allied attack that commenced afterwards was repelled by the Germans inflicting heavy casualties on the attackers. At around 0900 hours, with significant support from artillery and AT guns, the Allied troops took Fontana and took a firm stand by the south-eastern exit of Faicchio. This latter settlement was firmly held by the Germans by putting all their strength into action for the time being.

The left flank of the German combat outpost line west of the Monte Acero had to be pulled back to the Massa Nicolai–Fomlardi sector.

To the south of the mountain the Germans fought successful defensive battles, in which – according to the war diary of the *3. Panzergrenadier-Division* – especially the assault guns of *Panzer-Abteilung 103,* the field artillery and the multiple rocket-launchers excelled themselves.[44]

German fighter aircraft efficiently supported the defence from 1620 hours but five German bombs hit their own positions. As a result, battle group *'Haen'* lost one seriously and two slightly wounded men. The assault guns were also strafed by the aircraft but survived without sustaining any significant damage. A German fighter crashed nearby.

At around 1530 hours, the Allied combat vehicles attempted to cross the River Titerno north-east of Faicchio. The German artillery knocked out an AFV whereupon the others retreated. At around 1600 hours another Allied attack was launched but was halted by a German counterthrust. On the front line of the *I. Bataillon* of *Grenadier-Regiment (mot.) 8* Allied artillery fire started at 1645 hours. German reconnaissance patrols were repulsed by the Allies.

---

39 NARA T315, R173 (*3. Panzergrenadier-Division*), F000041.

40 See sketch-map of the fighting on 12 October 1943 in the Appendices.

41 NARA T315, R173 (*3. Panzergrenadier-Division*), F000042.

42 Dieckhoff, Gerhard: *3. Infanterie-Division – 3. Infanterie-Division (mot.) – 3. Panzergrenadier-Division* Cuxhaven, s.a., p. 254.

43 NARA T315, R173 (*3. Panzergrenadier-Division*), F000509.

44 NARA T315, R173 (*3. Panzergrenadier-Division*), F000045.

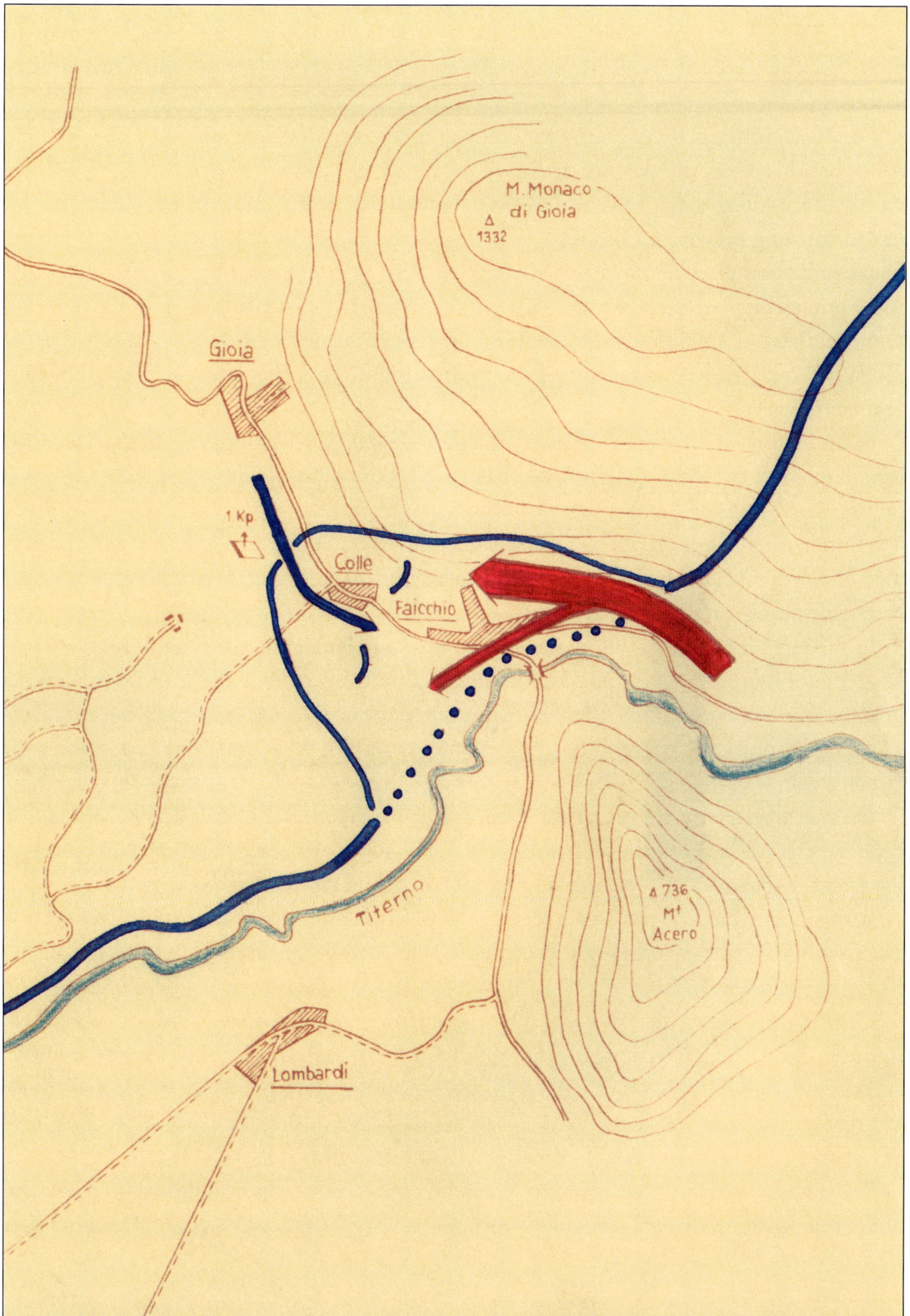

Situation map, 14 October 1943

On 15 October, battle group *'Haen'* repelled three Allied attacks that were partly supported by AFVs. The Germans knocked out two AFVs, shot down two aircraft, muted two artillery batteries and took seven prisoners.[45]

On 16 October at 0130 hours, an alert was ordered for the German troops because the Allies had breached the defence at the *1. Kompanie* of *Grenadier-Regiment (mot.) 8.* The attackers advanced tentatively behind the German rear guards and reconnaissance patrols in the morning hours. At around 0800 hours, about 50-60 Allied soldiers pressed towards Gioia, and another force of platoon strength climbed up the slopes north-east of Felicia. At 0900 hours *Panzer-Aufklärungs-Abteilung 103* engaged in a gun battle with an Allied group of 50 soldiers. At 1300 hours two Allied companies advanced from Audini towards Criscia. At Points 243 and 110, and through Santa Maria al Bagno, the Allies infiltrated forward very cautiously.

In the central sector of the *3. Panzergrenadier-Division* Allied troops advanced to the road fork 5km north of Cajazzo, but they were stopped there by the Germans who were supported by the assault guns of *Panzer-Abteilung 103.*[46]

On the other hand, on the right flank along the River Volturno, significant Allied forces (one or two companies) pursued the retreating Germans. The defenders knocked out an Allied reconnaissance armoured car here.

In the morning, Allied artillery shelled the area of Pasquale and the road fork 1km north of it. In addition, time and time again, larger calibre guns carried out surprise fire attacks into the depth of the German defences. Due to that, the wheeled vehicles of *Panzer-Abteilung 103* left the unit's command post at Gioia and assembled at a temporary command post established in Calvisi.

On that day, command of battle group *'Haen'* was taken over by *Major* Häckel. At that time the unit was made of the staff and *1.* and *3. Kompanie* of *Panzer-Abteilung 103,* as well as the *I.* and *II. Bataillon* of *Grenadier-Regiment (mot.) 8* and *Panzer-Aufklärungs-Abteilung 103.*

Battle group *'Häckel'* was put under command of battle group *'Moeller.'* Therefore the assault guns of *Panzer-Abteilung 103* could be employed in the whole defensive area of the *3. Panzergrenadier-Division.*[47]

On the night from the 16 to 17 October, battle group *'Moeller',* based on *Grenadier-Regiment (mot.) 20,* received orders from the division to quietly break contact with the enemy and defend the Hill 547 – Hill 593 – Hill 507 – south-eastern perimeter of Marco – River Volturno line 1.5km south-east of the Margherita Bridge during the day. The *2. Kompanie* of *Panzer-Abteilung 103* was subordinated to that battle group.[48]

The division withdrew battle group *'Häckel'* to the so-called 'Position Max', to the sector of the line River Volturno 1.5km south-east of the Margherita bridge – south foreground of Gaglione – Hill 194 – Criscia.[49]

45 NARA T315, R173 (*3. Panzergrenadier-Division*), F000464.

46 Dieckhoff, Gerhard: 3. Infanterie-Division – 3. Infanterie-Division (mot.) – 3. Panzergrenadier-*Division* Cuxhaven, s.a., p. 258.

47 Dieckhoff, Gerhard: 3. Infanterie-Division – 3. Infanterie-Division (mot.) – 3. Panzergrenadier-*Division* Cuxhaven, s.a., pp. 257-258.

48 NARA T315, R173 (*3. Panzergrenadier-Division*), F000461.

49 NARA T315, R173 (*3. Panzergrenadier-Division*), F000462.

On 18 October, the US 15th Infantry Regiment, attacking from the direction of Villa northwards through the hills, took Hill 330 in the southern foreground of Statigliano. Jumping off from there the Americans closed the two roads running between Latina and Pietramelara. The *3. Panzergrenadier-Division* put the *6.* and *8. Kompanien* of *Grenadier-Regiment (mot.) 29,* an armoured-car platoon of *Panzer-Aufklärungs-Abteilung 103* and one of the assault gun platoons (commander: *Leutnant* Zippel) of *Panzer-Abteilung 103* into action against them in the direction of Statigliano. The German battle group was supported only by a gun battery, which was unable to conduct fire through the hills. The assault guns and the armoured cars were unable to deploy on the narrow roads. Thus the German counterattack could only retake the eastern exit of Statigliano where it ground to a halt in the midst of the vicious American machine-gun and mortar fire.[50]

On 19 October, battle group *'Häckel'* continued its withdrawal. A new command post was set up in San Angelo de Alife.

Meanwhile, the staff of the division ordered the *1. Kompanie* of *Panzer-Abteilung 103* to the area of San Felice. The assault gun platoon *'Gehlen'* was sent into action as rear guard of the *II. Bataillon* of *Grenadier-Regiment (mot.) 8* along the San Potito–Piedimonte–Panella road. The assault gun platoon *'Johl'* took over the task of rear guard on the front line of the *I. Bataillon* of *Grenadier-Regiment (mot.) 8* along the River Volturno.

At around 1900 hours the *3. Kompanie* was already in its new positions in the area of San Angelo and Gioia. *Leutnant* Gehlen was given the task to be the last to retreat with the rear guard and issue orders to the pioneers to blow up the bridges and the buildings, especially in Piedimonte. Having carried out his tasks very thoroughly, the second lieutenant arrived at Panalla at 0900 hours.

On that day, on the front line of battle group *'Häckel'*, the Germans had to repulse attempts carried out by minor Allied reconnaissance patrols. However, the securing positions of the *3. Kompanie* were hammered by violent Allied surprise fire attacks.

During the next two days, the Allies continued to undertake reconnaissance missions but these were repelled again and again by the Germans. The positions held by the *3. Kompanie* remained under constant artillery fire.

On 20 October, the Allied troops tried to reconstruct the shattered road bridge south-east of Latina, in the area of Contra, while protected by 12 AFVs[51] but they were prevented in doing so by efficient fire from the assault guns of *Panzer-Abteilung 103* and some infantry guns.[52]

On 21 October, in the morning, Allied troops commenced an attack with a strength of one and a half companies on the left flank of battle group *'Häckel'*. It was repelled by the Germans with the support of assault gun platoon *'Heim'* which had been brought forward to the main combat line. At the same time, Allied reconnaissance patrols were forced back on the right flank. The assault gun platoon *'Johl'* took its share of the battle here.

---

50 Dieckhoff, Gerhard: 3. Infanterie-Division – *3. Infanterie-Division (mot.) – 3. Panzergrenadier-Division* Cuxhaven, s.a. p. 259.

51 Those were probably the AFVs of the US 751st Tank Battalion, which, providing support for the infantry penetrated Latina across Hill 207. *See* Dieckhoff, Gerhard: *3. Infanterie-Division – 3. Infanterie-Division (mot.) – 3. Panzergrenadier-Division* Cuxhaven, s.a., p. 260.

52 NARA T315, R173 (*3. Panzergrenadier-Division*), F000056.

The *3. Sturmgeschütz-Kompanie* was able to seal off an Allied penetration on the line of the *I. Bataillon* of *Grenadier-Regiment (mot.) 8,* drive German infantry that had left their positions back to the main combat line, and then from 1300 hours, together with elements of *Panzer-Aufklärungs-Abteilung 103* and *Grenadier-Regiment (mot.) 8* – with the support of 14 assault guns – restore the former front line with a counterthrust.[53]

Due to severe Allied artillery fire, the assault guns of *Panzer-Abteilung 103* were forced to retreat to their jump off positions. *Oberfeldwebel* Heinel was seriously wounded by shrapnel and died next day in the dressing station. Meanwhile the Americans made a rapid progress to San Angelo.[54]

During that time the *1. Kompanie* was in its readiness position, ready to launch a possible attack in a south-westerly direction. One of the assault guns (commander: *Leutnant* Gran) slid down the bridge of a stream and fell into the water. A recovery attempt began.[55]

On the night from 21 to 22 October, battle group *'Häckel'* resumed its withdrawal. The new command post was established in Raviscanina. During the procedure for breaking contact with the enemy, three StuG. IIIs of the *3. Sturmgeschütz-Kompanie* became bogged down due to extremely bad ground conditions and were unable to free themselves without assistance. However the three AFVs[56] were successfully recovered by the company despite the fact that the Allied troops had outflanked them on two sides. Moreover, one of the pursuing armoured cars was knocked out by the assault guns. Inside the vehicle the Germans found a portable American radio transceiver and several operational maps.

The Allied reconnaissance patrols got behind the retreating German infantry as early as the morning hours, and then tried to advance towards Raviscanina through the hills north of San Angelo in the afternoon. Therefore the assault gun platoon *'Grafe'* was drawn forward to San Angelo, but due to the very difficult terrain conditions the AFVs couldn't be put into action against the Allied infantry climbing up the hills. So, for want of a better plan of action, the assault gun platoon jumped off against the reconnaissance patrols that were pressing forward.

Having completed their withdrawal, they spent the night peacefully, apart from ceaseless harassing fire. The *3. Sturmgeschütz-Kompanie* took up a readiness position 1km west of Raviscanina. Meanwhile, the assault gun platoon *'Grafe'* was fighting in the sector of the *8. Kompanie* of *Grenadier-Regiment (mot.) 8* 1.5km to the south. In the evening, *Hauptmann* Heller, commander of the *2. Kompanie*, being away, submitted the following report:

'Dear Sir Mr Captain!

The company has been undertaking such arduous missions for days now, being the connecting link over and over. Yesterday, the anticipated armoured attack was launched by the enemy. Our position was rather unfavourable. The combat vehicles were Shermans and General Lees. In spite of that, Feldwebel *Fietz set a General Lee on fire and disabled another one with his shells.*

---

53 NARA T315, R173 (*3. Panzergrenadier-Division*), F000059.

54 Dieckhoff, Gerhard: 3. Infanterie-Division – *3. Infanterie-Division (mot.) – 3. Panzergrenadier-Division* Cuxhaven, s.a., p. 261.

55 *Kriegstagebuch der Panzer-Abteilung 103* (copy in author's possession), p. 39.

56 According to the war diary of the *3. Panzergrenadier-Division*, two assault guns were to be recovered. *See* NARA T315, R173 (*3. Panzergrenadier-Division*), F000060.

[The assault gun] of Feldwebel *Fietz was hit by a large calibre artillery shell. [The armour] was not penetreted. However, brackets were torn off in the fighting compartment. The members of the crew dismounted, then, after the fire was ceased, the assault gun was towed away. It is combat ready now.*

Another assault gun received a direct hit from above after having been hit three times by artillery fire. The crew members abandoned it after the third hit and so avoided certain death. The superstructure of the assault gun was totally torn apart. However it was successfully towed away, and now it is with the I. supply column of the company. I am glad, that we suffered no more casualties. It is my humble request, that this assault gun may be towed to the workshop by a prime mover. Otherwise we are quite well aside from the fact that we haven't had an hour's rest.[57]

On the night from 22 to 23 October, the situation was calm. At dawn the Allied troops attempted to press forward yet again through the hills north of San Angelo, as well as on the hills in the area of Vecchio. Therefore the *3. Kompanie* took up positions from which they could keep the slopes under fire. Nevertheless, the Allies were able to move forward on the mountainous terrain with diminished fields of view and pose a threat to the flanks of battle group *'Häckel'*. Due to that, retreat was ordered again.

In the sector of the *2. Kompanie,* fighting at some distance from the bulk of *Panzer-Abteilung 103,* the Allied AFVs launched another attack in the afternoon. The assault guns of the company let the AFVs come close before destroying three Shermans, whereupon the other AFVs left the field in panic.[58] It is very important to note that this was the first time in the Italian theatre that the crews of the assault guns of *Panzer-Abteilung 103* had to face the fact that the German infantry had let the Allied AFVs roll over their positions with cold-blooded indifference and waited for the assault guns in their firing positions further back to open fire. The acting commander of the supported *12. Kompanie* of *Grenadier-Regiment (mot.) 29, Leutnant* Wachsmuth, wrote the following letter of gratitude to the commander of the *2. Kompanie*:

'Herr Kaptain Heller! The 12. Kompanie expresses its gratitude to you Herr Kaptain, for your support. Your soldiers prevented the breakthrough, and our soldiers overcame their fear of AFVs. On behalf of the 12. Kompanie I thank you ever so much.'[59]

By morning 24 October, the new command post had been established in Ailano. In a short while *Hauptmann* Heller arrived and reported, that the *2. Kompanie*, relieved from assignment with battle group *'Moeller'* the previous evening, was on the march back to its parent unit.

57 *Kriegstagebuch der Panzer-Abteilung 103* (copy in author's possession), pp. 40-41.

58 According to the war diary of the *3. Panzergrenadier-Division,* the Allies launched their attack following an artillery preparation at around 1500 hours with 16 AFVs bypassing Baia e Latina from two sides. Besides the three knocked-out Sherman tanks, the Germans blew up a fourth AFV left behind by its crew. *See* NARA T315, R173 (*3. Panzergrenadier-Division*), F000061. German reconnaissance identified forces of the 751st Tank Battalion supporting the US 3rd Infantry Division in the area. *See* NARA T315, R173 (*3. Panzergrenadier-Division*), F000062. During interrogation of POWs, the Germans learned that around 24 October the American independent tank battalion had 46 combat-ready Shermans with an additional five repairable in one day, and by that time it had lost 14 AFVs. In addition to that, the American infantry was also supported by the 601st Tank-Destroyer Battalion with 34 M10 tank destroyers in this sector. *See* NARA T315, R173 (*3. Panzergrenadier-Division*), F001047.

59 *Kriegstagebuch der Panzer-Abteilung 103* (copy in author's possession), p. 42.

The *2. Kompanie* was quartered in the area of Pratella and was held in reserve. The *3. Kompanie* took up positions 1.5km south of Ailano. Following the orders received, the assault gun platoons *'Grafe'* and *'Heim'* having pressed by the enemy, retreated together with the rear guards of the infantry. The assault gun platoon *'Gehlen'* was dispatched to the *1. Kompanie*.

In the morning hours the Allied artillery enfiladed the new positions of battle group *'Häckel'*. The reconnaissance patrols, one by one, retreated after their first engagement with the enemy. From noon till the evening hours violent artillery fire was poured mainly onto the connecting routes running in the valley of the River Lete.

On 25 October, in the morning, the positions of the *3. Kompanie* were under fierce artillery harassing fire. Battle group *'Häckel'* was unable to re-establish contact with the Allies, broken the previous evening, despite sending out infantry reconnaissance patrols. However, the Allied artillery poured harassing fire all day onto the road fork south of Ailano, the bottleneck at Pratella and on the settlement itself. There the *2. Kompanie* suffered a few wounded and several assault guns were damaged.

According to orders issued by the division at 1400 hours on the same day, the *1. Kompanie* was to be available for the division commander in the northern foreground of Greci, so that they could be sent into action along the road running north from the railway station of Vairano, should the Allies achieve a breakthrough.[60]

On 26 October at 0530 hours the Allied artillery started firing again. The concentration of artillery fire was laid down mainly on the area of Ailano. The harassing fire was increased to destructive effect within a few minutes.

Shells were showered in till 0730 hours, and then the furious volume of fire slackened off before 0930 hours. Luckily for the Germans, they had excellent cover in Ailano and its vicinity and, consequently, *Panzer-Abteilung 103* suffered no casualties.

The 2nd Battalion of the US 135th Infantry Regiment launched an attack with a two-company-strength force on the left flank of battle group *'Häckel'* to take Hill 235 2km south of Ailano. The assault gun platoon *'Heim'* was sent against them, which – together with the *3. Kompanie* of *Grenadier-Regiment (mot.) 8*[61] – repulsed the attempt. To the right of the highway, minor advances were made, but these were also stopped by the Germans. Following this, the Allied troops dug in about 300m from the German main combat line – the Germans had therefore temporarily halted the advance of the US troops in the valley of the River Volturno.

In the early afternoon, the command post of battle group *'Häckel'* found itself under machine-gun fire from a nearby hill. It became obvious that the Allies had infiltrated behind the German positions and had taken advantage of gaps that had opened up on the German's sparsely occupied flanks. Although they were under attack from only insignificant forces, the command post was prepared for defence. It was most awkward for the Germans that the route leading to the command post was exposed to enemy machine-gun fire. The Germans scrutinized the slopes for hours but were unable to identify the firing position of the machine gun. At around 1700 hours, the reconnaissance and counterintelligence staff officer of the

60 NARA T315, R173 (*3. Panzergrenadier-Division*), F000399.

61 Dieckhoff, Gerhard: *3. Infanterie-Division – 3. Infanterie-Division (mot.) – 3. Panzergrenadier-Division* Cuxhaven, s.a., p. 262.

division informed the battle group by radio that the Allies had located the position of the command post and that the infiltrating unit operating on their flank possibly had orders to eliminate it.

As a countermeasure, the Germans sent two platoons of the *6. Kompanie* of *Grenadier-Regiment (mot.) 8* to carry out securing tasks, together with the reconnaissance and AA machine-cannon platoons of *Panzer-Abteilung 103* and several command tanks. They took up positions from which they were able to keep the whole area of the hills under fire. However, so far the Allies hadn't made any attempt to threaten the command post.

On 27 October, in the early hours, noise made by AFVs were reported from the left flank of battle group *'Häckel'*. At 0530 hours the Allied artillery resumed its attack on Ailano and the German main combat line. At 0700 hours Allied AFVs pressed forward on the left flank. Assault gun platoon *'Heim'* – in cooperation with the *14. Kompanie* of *Grenadier-Regiment (mot.) 8* – knocked out a Sherman tank.

At around 1000 hours, the German forces securing Hill 559 reported that the Allies had taken advantage of the early morning mist and had taken the hill. Thus the threat to the battle group command post became even more grave. The Germans sent reconnaissance patrols with sufficient firepower to be able to fend off a possible flank attack. Meanwhile the Allied artillery carried out violent surprise attacks on Ailano, Pratella and the connecting route.

At 1500 hours, *Oberleutnant* Gerhard Johl – who commanded *3. Kompanie* during the short absence of *Hauptmann* Fisher – carried out an attack on an Allied jump-off position (an infantry company with two Sherman tanks). Due to the disadvantageous firing positions taken up by the assault guns, the first lieutenant decided to advance and fight down the assembling forces of the Allies with 12 StuG. III assault guns[62]. The assault guns achieved their objective of destroying the jump-off position and also knocked out one of the Sherman tanks. However the German company did not escape without loss: *Oberfeldwebel* Seitzinger was killed by a shell fragment and his assault gun was damaged. The StuG. III of *Oberfeldwebel* Stanni took a direct hit but the crew was able to crawl out unharmed. The assault gun of *Fahnenjunker-Oberfeldwebel* Grafe also received a hit and the assault gun commander was wounded.

In the evening battle group *'Häckel'* was withdrawn again to the so-called 5th intermediate line *(Zwischenlinie V)*. In the new defensive area the defensive positions were established as series of dispersed strongpoints without a continuous main combat line.

The *3. Kompanie* was employed as a whole in the area of Giorlano, along the highway. The *2. Kompanie* was in reserve 2km north of Pte. Reale. A new battle group command post was established at the southern exit of Capriati.

On the night from 27 to 28 October, the *II. Bataillon* of *Grenadier-Regiment (mot.) 8* was detached from the battle group and the command of the unit passed from *Major* Häckel to *Hauptmann* Haen.

At that time the battle group was made up of *Panzer-Abteilung 103* and *Panzer-Aufklärungs-Abteilung 103.*[63] The day passed without event.

62 Dieckhoff, Gerhard: 3. Infanterie-Division – *3. Infanterie-Division (mot.) – 3. Panzergrenadier-Division* Cuxhaven, s.a., p. 263.

63 Dieckhoff, Gerhard: *3. Infanterie-Division – 3. Infanterie-Division (mot.) – 3. Panzergrenadier-Division* Cuxhaven, s.a., p. 264.

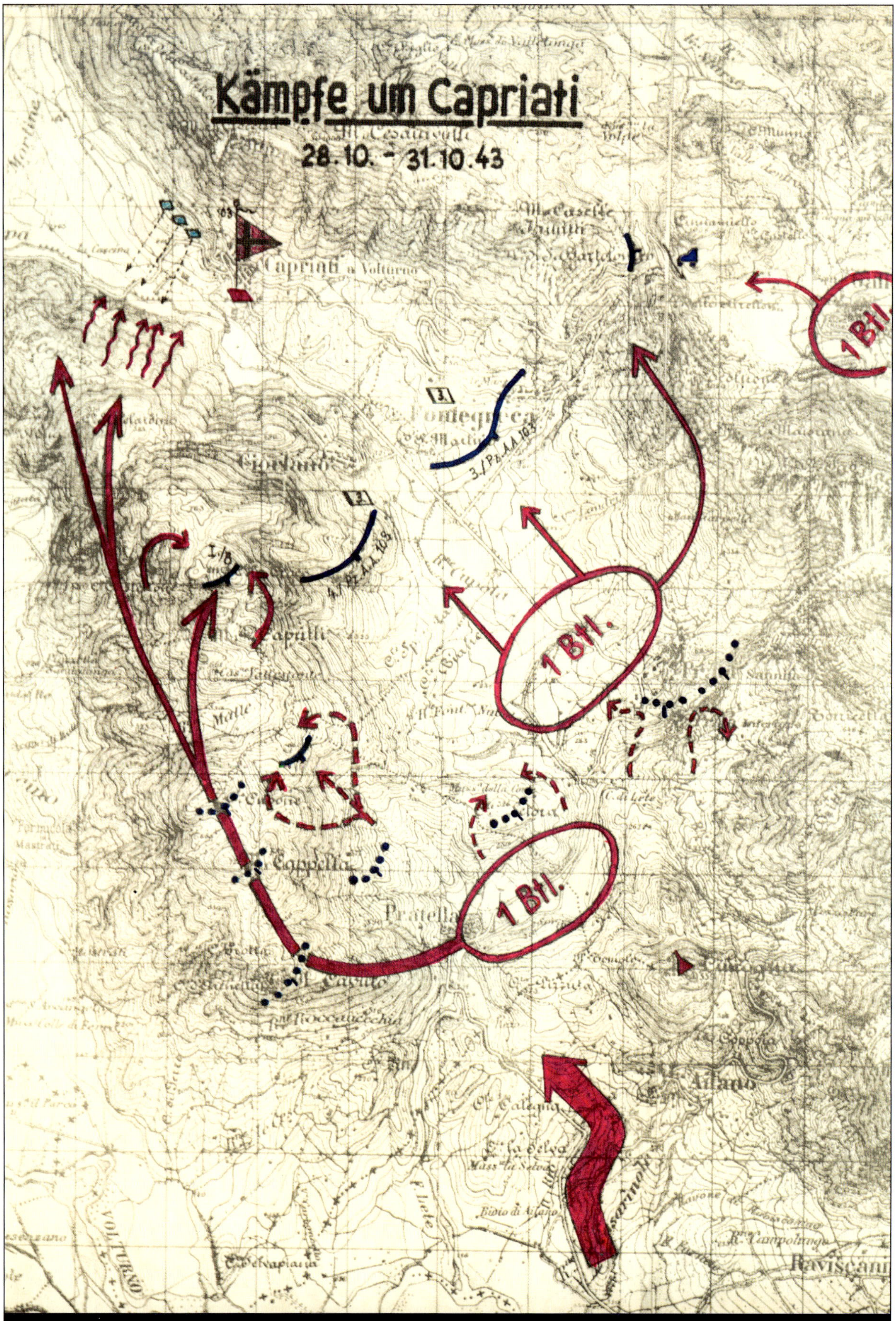

Situation map, 18-31 October 1943

On the night from 28 to 29 October, assault gun platoon *'Heim'* was sent into action on the highway running between Capriati and Callo. In the morning, the Allied troops launched attacks on the right and left flanks of the battle group but their attempts, carried out by weak forces, were repelled by the Germans. In the afternoon the attacks continued: this time two companies dashed forward on each flank following a thorough artillery preparation. Hard pressed by the Allies on their right flank, the Germans retreated. However, on the left flank, in the area of Prata, the light APCs of the *3. Kompanie* of *Panzer-Aufklärungs-Abteilung 103* held on and repulsed the two-company-strength attacking infantry with the support of assault gun platoon *'Heim'*.[64]

On 30 October, the Allied troops made no attempt to attack in the sector of battle group *'Haen'*. At around 1330 the corps commander visited the command post with *Generalleutnant* Gräser, the division commander, and having been informed about the situation, he expressed his satisfaction with the achievements of the battle group.

In the afternoon, a report was received according to which the company sent to cover the right flank on Hills 729 and 660 was annihilated in a surprise attack. As a result, the right flank of the battle group became exposed and consequently ordered to retreat to the 6th intermediate line *(Zwischenlinie VI)* during the night hours. On the other hand, the *3. Kompanie* remained in its previous position for the time being.

On 31 October, in the early morning, the Allied troops launched yet another attack with fierce artillery support on the new positions of battle group *'Haen'*. However, the attempts were repelled again by the Germans and their own infantry on the left flank was supported by assault gun platoon *'Heim'*. During the noon hours, the American troops came around Hill 811 south of Capriati and, by so doing, had succeeded in making another deep penetration into the flank of the German battle group. A German infantry company, sent into action without a delay, was not able to fend off this danger entirely. With this, the battle group command post was exposed to American reconnaissance and shortly afterwards it did indeed receive extremely accurate artillery fire.

Simultaneously, the Allies made rapid progress on the left flank through Callo towards San Benedetta. The German positions set up in the valley were shelled by Allied artillery.

Major Haen sent the assault guns of the *3. Kompanie* of *Panzer-Abteilung 103* and the light APCs of the *3. Kompanie* of *Panzer-Aufklärungs-Abteilung 103* to defend Capriati. However, the latter company had only about 50 combat-ready soldiers left, and the assault guns were unable to support them effectively due to their disadvantageous firing positions. As a result, battle group *'Haen'* was forced to retreat to the northern foreground of Capriati.[65] Afterwards, the *3. Kompanie* of the *Panzer-Abteilung 103* took up positions with its assault guns on the highway running between Capriati and the northern bridge of the Volturno River.

---

64 Dieckhoff, Gerhard: 3. *Infanterie-Division – 3. Infanterie-Division (mot.) – 3. Panzergrenadier-Division* Cuxhaven, s.a., p. 264.

65 Dieckhoff, Gerhard: 3. Infanterie-Division – *3. Infanterie-Division (mot.) – 3. Panzergrenadier-Division* Cuxhaven, s.a. p. 265.

Situation map, 31 October - 1 November 1943

According to the divisional order as of 1200 hours, the *1. Kompanie* of *Panzer-Abteilung 103,* attached to battle group *'Schultzendorff'*, based on the *I. Bataillon* of *Grenadier-Regiment (mot.) 29,* was fighting in the valley of the Volturno River, and the *3. Kompanie* was operating in battle group *'Haen'* along the highway between Prata and Capriati, and to the west of it.[66]

In the late afternoon, *Major* Haen prevented a flanking attack launched westwards by the Allies and inflicted such heavy losses on them that they had to cease their advance.

Having been drawn forward in the course of the night, the *2. Kompanie* was placed behind the *3. Kompanie.* The new command post of the battle group was established 1.5km south of the northern bridge, at Point 207.

Changes also occurred in the chain of command. The commander of the *2. Kompanie, Hauptmann* Heller, was ordered to Paris to attend a course for commanders. The company's command was taken over by *Oberleutnant* Häusser. His previous assignment as commander of the staff company was given to *Leutnant* Gran.

On 1 November, the Allied forces resumed their advance through Capriati and to the east of it in the early hours. In the morning, the Germans observed the arrival of a great number of American supply trucks. The Allied force fighting on the hills north of Capriati was also growing bigger and stronger.

Around noon, the positions of battle group *'Haen'* were attacked by a one-and-a-half battalion-strength Allied force.[67] The assault guns of *Panzer-Abteilung 103* were unable to take up proper firing positions in the extremely rugged terrain which was thickly overgrown with vegetation. The concept of having lines of communication established with all heavy weapons (the *II. Abteilung* of *Panzer-Artillerie-Regiment 3,* two batteries of *Nebelwerfer-Regiment 71* and an 8.8cm AA-battery), in the keeping with the orders of the commander of the battle group, proved effective. As a result of this precaution, the fire of all the supporting batteries could be concentrated on a single, threatened point. The effectiveness of this shelling was enhanced by ground attacks carried out by German fighters. The Allied attack failed, allowing battle group *'Haen'* to retreat undisturbed after nightfall to the 'Bernhardt Line' southwest of Venafro.

66 NARA T315, R173 (*3. Panzergrenadier-Division*), F000364.

67 Reconnaissance of the *3. Panzergrenadier-Division* identified elements of the 133rd Infantry Regiment of US 34th Infantry Division, in which, at least partly, American citizens of Japanese ancestry fought. *See* NARA T315, R173 (*3. Panzergrenadier-Division*), F000350.

4

In the "Bernhardt Line"

On 2 November, battle group *'Haen'* – which included the *I. Bataillon* of *Grenadier-Regiment (mot.) 8,* the light Sd. Kfz. 250 APCs of the *4. Kompanie* of *Panzer-Aufklärungs-Abteilung 103* as well as most of *Panzer-Abteilung 103* – was given the task of defending the ridge between Hills 456 and 385 4km south-west of Venafro. The *1. Kompanie* of the armoured unit was fighting in the area of Venafro and Pozzilli under command of battle group *'Schultzendorff'.*[68]

During their retreat the *2. Kompanie* was subordinated to *Panzer-Aufklärungs-Abteilung 103.* The *3. Kompanie* was sent to action in the area of Point 165 to perform security duties southwards and westwards. The new battle group command post was established first 2km west-south-west of Venafro, in an olive grove, but then was relocated on 2 November to Ceppagna.

On the night from 2 to 3 November, the *3. Kompanie* was withdrawn to the southern and south-western perimeter of the olive grove west-south-west of Venafro because the Allies had got behind the right flank of battle group *'Haen'* – again unobtrusively, by moving across the mountainous terrain of Monte Cesima under limited view. To fend off the flank attack, the *III. Bataillon* of *Fallschirmjäger-Regiment 6* was ordered to the area of Monte Cesima.

During the day the Allied artillery carried out violent surprise fire-attacks on the German positions. The intensive German combat reconnaissance discovered that the Allied forces were pressing forward in the area of Ponte Reale and also on the hillside south-west of Pipirossi.

On 4 November, in the morning hours, significant Allied forces[69] launched an attack from the direction of Ponte Reale towards Venafro. The *4. Kompanie* of *Panzer-Aufklärungs-Abteilung 103,* located in the olive grove there, was pushed forward in the direction of Il Canale with securing tasks to perform. Assault gun platoon *'Johl'* provided support for the Sd. Kfz. 250 APCs, from the area of Point 170. However that sector was fully observed by the Allies, so they immediately detected the movement of the armoured reconnaissance company and placed the Germans under fire. The German company ground to a halt.

68 NARA T315, R173 (*3. Panzergrenadier-Division*), F000074.

69 In these days the *3. Panzergrenadier-Division* fought against forces of the 3rd, 34th and 45th Infantry Divisions assigned to the US VI Corps.

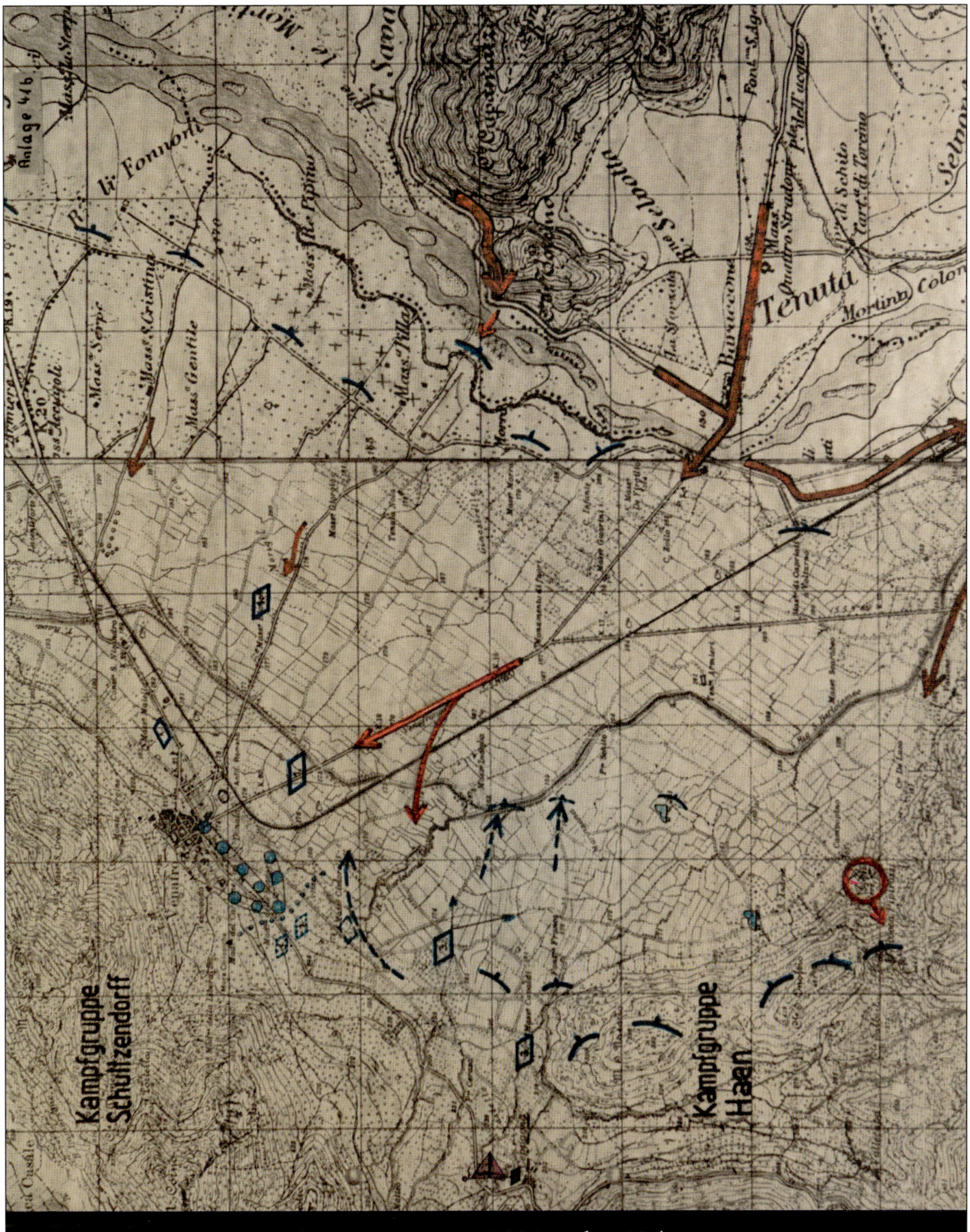

Situation map, 2-3 November 1943

At 0645 hours, the *3. Panzergrenadier-Division* reported that the assault guns of *Panzer-Abteilung 103* were also ordered to carry out a counterthrust on the American forces attacking in the area of Ponte Reale, 4km north-east of the bridge across the Volturno River.[70]

70 NARA T315, R173 (*3. Panzergrenadier-Division*), F000331.

At around 1100 hours the Allied troops approached Venafro. The assault guns of the *1. Kompanie*, in cooperation with the *2. Kompanie* of *Grenadier-Regiment (mot.) 29*, commenced but failed to achieve an effective counterthrust. Moreover, the commander of the grenadier company was killed.[71] As a result, to avoid becoming isolated, battle group *'Schultzendorff'* (including the *1. Kompanie* of *Panzer-Abteilung 103*) had to retreat through the settlement to battle group *'Haen'* by orders from the division. During this withdrawal the division's commander, Generalleutnant Grässer arrived and than he drove forward towards the front line in a command tank of the Panzer-Abteilung 103. With his consent, battle group *'Schultzendorff'* (including the *1. Sturmgeschütz-Kompanie*) was sent into action along the highway running through a pass 2km south-west of Venafro. Battle group *'Haen'* defended its positions on the southern perimeter of the settlement.

During the next counterthrust, a group of assault guns penetrated the area of Venafro again and obtained excellent reconnaissance information but, without supporting infantry, the Germans were unable to exploit this success.[72] In the evening the Allies constructed a bridge suitable for AFVs to cross the river in the area of Venafro.[73]

The Allied artillery bombardment began in the early morning hours and lasted all day. Meanwhile the command post of the battle group was also shelled heavily, as was the road running through the pass at Ceppagna.

In the evening battle group *'Haen'* received orders to retreat through the pass to the 'Bernhardt Line', which was already occupied. With these orders, every subordinate relationship was ended. *Panzer-Abteilung 103* – temporarily without its *2. Kompanie* – was quartered in its designated location in Cervaro.

On the same day the *2. Kompanie* came under command of *Grenadier-Regiment (mot.) 29.*[74]

On 5 November, in the evening, the *3. Panzergrenadier-Division* prepared an attack in the area of Pozzilli to occupy the former German main combat line. In the course of these preparations the *2. Kompanie* of *Panzer-Abteilung 103,* regrouped from the area of Filignano, made itself ready for combat subordinated to *Panzergrenadier-Regiment 9,*[75] but was required to be ready for deployment on request to the sector of *Grenadier-Regiment (mot.) 29.*[76] In the end, the planned action was terminated.

On 6 November, the armoured unit performed maintenance on its worn out vehicles. The *2. Kompanie* had seven combat-ready StuG. IIIs in the area of Acquafondata.[77]

On 7 November, the *1. Kompanie* with five combat-ready assault guns – subordinated to *Grenadier-Regiment (mot.) 8* – had already taken up its designated position on the 'Bernhardt Line'. One assault gun platoon was sent to the curve in the road at Monte Rotondo, under the command of *Oberleutnant der Reserve* Hinzpeter. Assault gun platoon *'Gehlen'* established defensive positions in the sector held by the troops of *Major* Häckel between Monte Lungo and Hill 371.

71 NARA T315, R173 (*3. Panzergrenadier-Division*), F000078.
72 NARA T315, R173 (*3. Panzergrenadier-Division*), F000078.
73 Dieckhoff, Gerhard: 3. Infanterie-Division – *3. Infanterie-Division (mot.) – 3. Panzergrenadier-Division* Cuxhaven, s.a., p. 271.
74 NARA T315, R173 (*3. Panzergrenadier-Division*), F000325.
75 The assault gun company was to choose positions, from where it was able to carry out even field artillery tasks.
76 NARA T315, R173 (*3. Panzergrenadier-Division*), F000309.
77 NARA T315, R173 (*3. Panzergrenadier-Division*), F000298.

On that day the *2. Kompanie* had eight and the *3. Kompanie* seven combat-ready StuG. III assault guns.[78]

On 8 November, the day passed more or less quietly, except for the fact that Allied artillery fire forced assault gun platoon *'Hinzpeter'* to withdraw 1km and take up new positions.

On 9 November, one *Sturmgeschütz-Kompanie* – possibly the *1. Kompanie* of *Panzer-Abteilung 103* – carried out artillery tasks in the area of M. Lungo. The other – probably the 3. *Kompanie* – was employed south of San Vittore in a blocking position to defend the main route, and to fend off any Allied AFVs that made an attempt to break through. On the same day, the *1. Kompanie* had five and the *3. Kompanie* 10 combat-ready assault guns.[79]

The *2. Kompanie* sent into action in the area of Acquafondata was withdrawn from the front line at around 1600 hours and received orders to move into the area of Cervaro in the evening.[80]

The assault gun platoon *'Gehlen'* provided support for the infantry during their attack on Hill 371, where the Allies had broken through. Thus the Allies observed the positions of the assault guns, and placed them under heavy artillery fire. On the front line of the assault gun platoon *'Hinzpeter'* the Allies commenced an attack, following artillery preparation with a barrage on Monte Rotondo, and occupied the hill.

The *2. Kompanie* was detached from *Grenadier-Regiment (mot.) 29* on that day, and then having started off from their previous deployment position at 1600 hours, they reached the designated quartering area of *Panzer-Abteilung 103* at Cervaro.

The *3. Kompanie* was brought forward to the 'Bernhardt Line' as early as on the night from 8 to 9 November.

On 10 November, the tactical situation was the same. The Allied artillery continued its harassing fire. *Oberleutnant* Johl supported the attack of the *3. Kompanie* of *Panzergrenadier-Regiment 104*[81] with two StuG. III assault guns.

In the afternoon the Allies commenced an attack on the southern part of M. Lungo with a two-company strength force and took Hill 283. However, they were unable to press forward from there, since the Germans, putting their last reserves into action and with the artillery fire support of the assault guns, halted them.[82]

The Allied air activity, that had been limited to sporadic reconnaissance missions due to bad weather conditions, became intensive again on that day. Towards nightfall the fighter-bombers attacked Cervaro, and cast bombs on the camping grounds of the assault gun companies as well as on the positions of the AA automatic cannon platoon.

On the night from 10 to 11 November, the *2. Kompanie*, held in divisional reserve, finished its short period of rest and maintenance of its vehicles, and moved to the 'Bernhardt Line'.

---

78 NARA T315, R173 (*3. Panzergrenadier-Division*), F000284.
79 NARA T315, R173 (*3. Panzergrenadier-Division*), F000268.
80 NARA T315, R173 (*3. Panzergrenadier-Division*), F000090.
81 The regiment belonged to the *15. Panzergrenadier-Division.*
82 NARA T315, R173 (*3. Panzergrenadier-Division*), F000097.

Situation map, 8-10 November 1943

On 12 November, the assault gun platoon *'Hinzpeter'* was relieved, leaving only the assault guns of *Leutnant* Gehlen remaining in their positions. The assault guns acting as artillery in the area of San Pietro were temporarily subordinated to *Artillerie-Regiment (mot.) 3.*[83]

According to the orders issued by the division, the *2. Kompanie* with its assault guns and the *4. (leichte) SPW Kompanie* (light APC company) of *Panzer-Aufklärungs-Abteilung 103* had to be ready to march at a 20 minutes' notice from 0530 hours.[84]

On 13 November, *Panzer-Abteilung 103* put command tanks and assault guns at the German artillery's disposal. These were deployed on the terrain with the limited aim of facilitating communications between the advanced artillery observers and the batteries.

In the evening the *3. Panzergrenadier-Division* requested 20 shafts for the traversing and elevating mechanism each of the assault guns' mechanisms for traversing and elevating from the superior *XIV. Panzerkorps.*[85]

On 14 November, although battle group *'Häckel'* was pulled out of the front line, the assault gun platoon *'Gehlen'* was subordinated to the battalion that had arrived to relieve it. However, the platoon was withdrawn at night instead. During the withdrawal, due to bad weather conditions, one of the assault guns was bogged down and, despite the joint efforts of the pioneer and recovery platoons, it couldn't be towed away.

On 16 November, elements of the *3. Panzergrenadier-Division* – including *Panzer-Abteilung 103* – came under the command of the *29. Panzergrenadier-Division* until the forces of the latter division arrived to take over the positions.[86]

From 14 to 17 November, the unit handed over a total of 24 StuG. III assault guns to *Panzer-Abteilung 129.*[87] By so doing, *Panzer-Abteilung 103* had only 14 assault guns left.[88] This implies that, of the 42 StuG. III assault guns originally issued, only four were written off as total losses.

On 18 November, the unit – together with other units of the *3. Panzergrenadier-Division* – was relieved and withdrawn from the front line. The tasks and quartering area of *Panzer-Abteilung 103* were taken over by *Panzer-Abteilung 129.* Following that, the unit took up its quarters south-west of Rome, and its command post was established in Nemi.[89]

On 19 November, the division issued orders to *Panzer-Abteilung 103* to reconnoitre the area to find out how to involve the fire power of the assault guns in the defensive-fire plan of the coastal defences.[90]

On 20 November, the staff of the division announced by telephone that *Panzer-Abteilung 103* would soon take over 23 assault guns from *Panzer-Regiment 2.*

83 NARA T315, R173 (*3. Panzergrenadier-Division*), F000108.

84 NARA T315, R173 (*3. Panzergrenadier-Division*), F000249.

85 NARA T315, R173 (*3. Panzergrenadier-Division*), F000236.

86 NARA T315, R173 (*3. Panzergrenadier-Division*), F000112.

87 *Panzer-Abteilung 129* was the *29. Panzergrenadier-Division*'s own armoured unit.

88 *Kriegstagebuch der Panzer-Abteilung 103* (copy in author's possession), p. 52.

89 According to the war diary of the *3. Panzergrenadier-Division, Panzer-Abteilung 103* would have started its march to Ostia on 17 November 1943 with special duty to perform, subordinated to *Panzer-Regiment 26*, then it would have arrived at its new quartering area on 18 November. *See* NARA T315, R173 (*3. Panzergrenadier-Division*), F000113. Unfortunately there is no detailed description of that action either in the division's war diary, or in that of the armoured unit (it is not even mentioned in the latter). In the end, the armoured unit set off at 0600 hours on 18 November 1943.

90 NARA T315, R173 (*3. Panzergrenadier-Division*), F000198.

Quartering area of Panzer-Abteilung 103 on 19 November 1943

On 21 November, the maintenance detachment of the *1. Kompanie* returned and reported that they were still unable to tow away the assault gun of the assault gun platoon *'Gehlen',* which had become bogged down a week before. On the same day *Panzer-Abteilung 103* was ordered to relocate again. This time the designated quartering area was in the area of Bracciano and the command post was established in Oriolo.

On 23 November, in the evening, *Panzer-Abteilung 103* had only three combat-ready assault guns, according to a report submitted by the *3. Panzergrenadier-Division.*[91]

On 25 November, the workshop platoon reported that, at last, the assault gun that had become stuck on 14 November had been successfully recovered. During the last days of the month, soldiers who had distinguished themselves in combat received their well-earned decorations.

At the end of November, 13 assault guns arrived from *Panzer-Regiment 2.* Five of them were given to the *1. Kompanie* and eight were delivered to the *3. Kompanie.*

On 30 November, another 10 assault guns were delivered to the unit, but for the time being they were operating in the area of Chieti. Having returned from the front line, the companies of *Panzer-Abteilung 103* had the following armoured strength:

- *1. Kompanie* (11 assault guns),
- *2. Kompanie* (13 assault guns),
- *3. Kompanie* (13 assault guns).[92]

Meanwhile *Oberfeldwebel* Heim from the *3. Kompanie* received the German Cross in Gold for his merit shown in combat, especially during the Battle of Stalingrad.

On 1 December, according to a report on combat strength submitted by its division[93], *Panzer-Abteilung 103* had only five combat-ready StuG. III assault guns left, as well as two command Panzer III tanks (with 5cm guns). The workshop platoon was busy carrying out short-term repairs to 17 assault guns and a command fighting vehicle.[94] Another 15 assault guns needed longer-term repairs.

According to figures relating to **2 December,** *1. and 2. Kompanien* each had eight assault guns and the *3. Kompanie* possessed six assault guns.[95]

Panzer-Abteilung 103 spent the first half of December preparing their newly received assault guns for combat while stationed at their designated quartering area in the vicinity of Oriolo and Manziana.

On 5 December, the *1. Kompanie* of *schwere Panzerjäger-Abteilung 525* with its 14 Hornisse tank destroyers came under the command of the *3. Panzergrenadier-Division.*[96]

---

91 NARA T315, R173 (*3. Panzergrenadier-Division*), F000191.

92 *Kriegstagebuch der Panzer-Abteilung 103* (copy in author's possession), pp. 53-54.

93 Other armoured elements of the *3. Panzergrenadier-Division* besides *Panzer-Abteilung 103* were the follows: *I. Abteilung* of *Artillerie-Regiment (mot.) 3* with 17×10.5cm Wespe self-propelled howitzers, *Panzer-Aufklärungs-Abteilung 103* with the 1. (wheeled) reconnaissance armoured car company, the 2. (half-track) reconnaissance armoured car company, the 3. and 4. (light APC) company, the 5. (armoured) heavy weapon company, and *Grenadier-Regiment (mot.) 8* and *29* with a regimental 15cm heavy self-propelled infantry gun company (with six AFVs each) respectively. *See* NARA T315, R173 (*3. Panzergrenadier-Division*), F000172.

94 NARA T315, R173 (*3. Panzergrenadier-Division*), F000170.

95 NARA T315, R173 (*3. Panzergrenadier-Division*), F000172.

96 NARA T315, R173 (*3. Panzergrenadier-Division*), F000116.

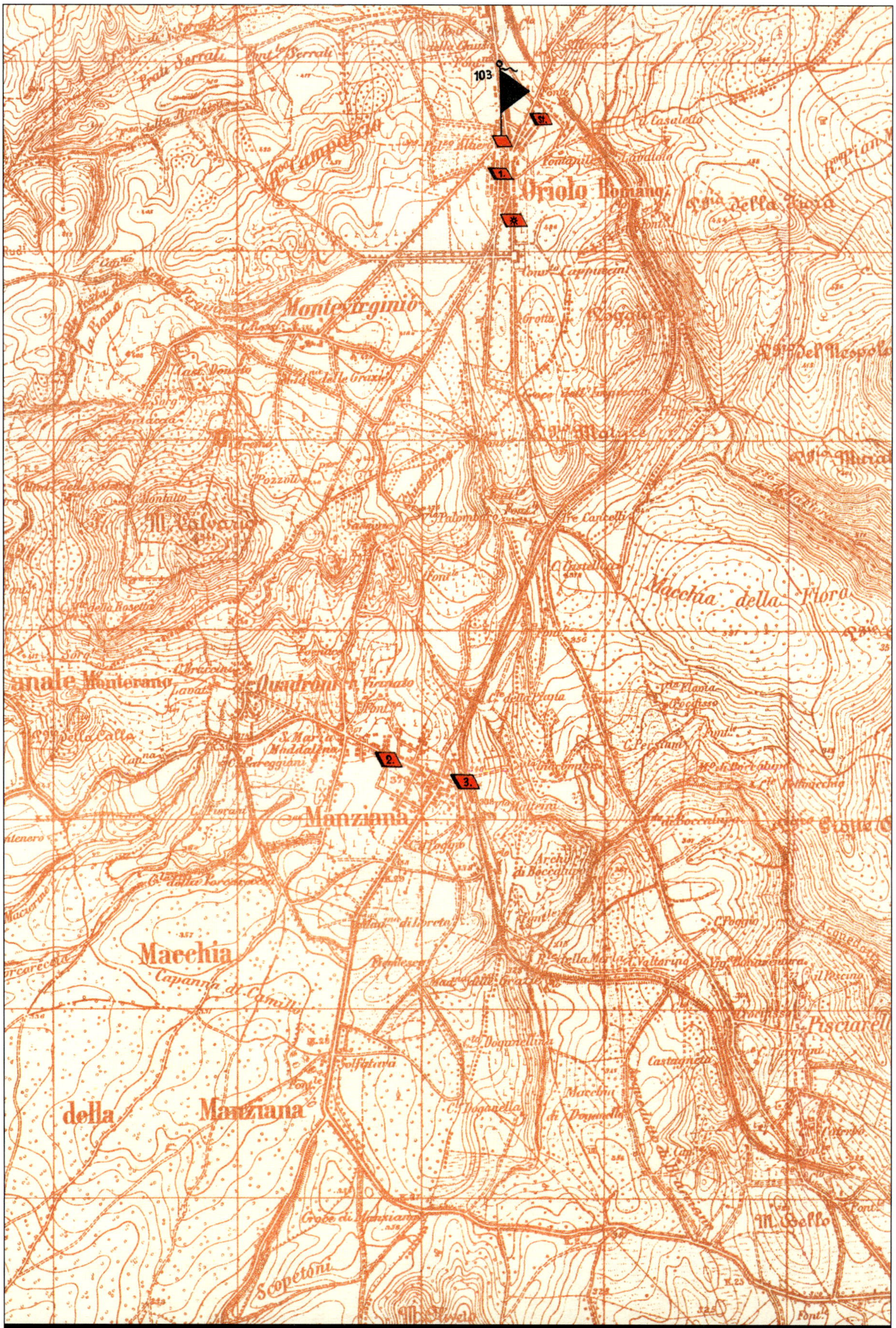

Quartering area of Panzer-Abteilung 103 on 21 November 1943

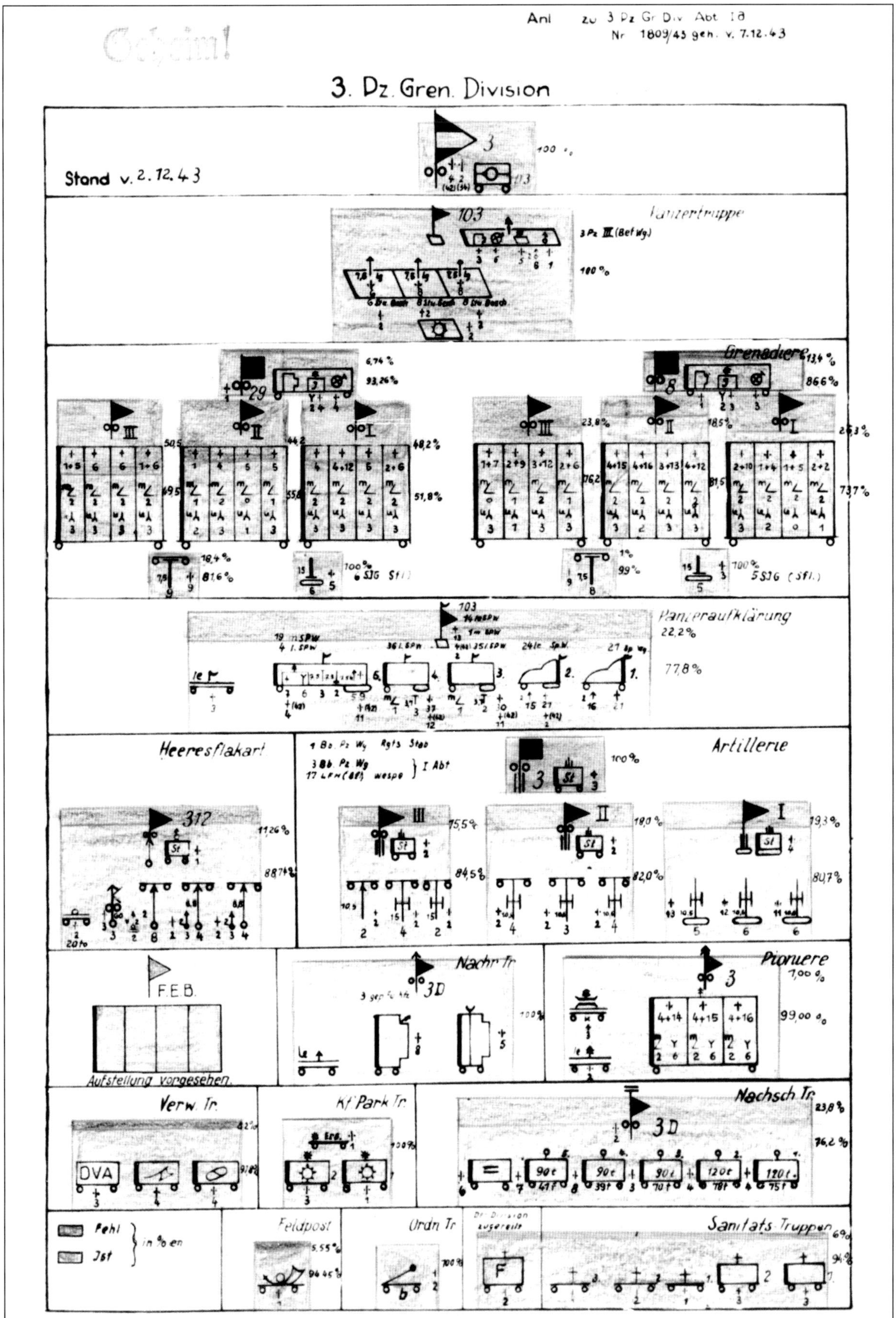

Order of battle of the 3. Panzergrenadier-Division on 7 December 1943

On 10 December, *Oberfeldwebel* Heim was promoted to *Hauptfeldwebel* and at the same time he was transferred to the unit's staff company.

The adjutant of *Panzer-Abteilung 103, Leutnant* Schwäpenheuer, was ordered to Burg bei Magdeburg to attend a course there for adjutants of assault gun units from 14 to 19 December, 1943.

On 18 December, at 0715 hours the division ordered alert level II. The units were notified within 15 minutes. At 0755 hours the combat echelons of *Panzer-Abteilung 103* reported that they were ready to march. The division called off the alert by telephone at 0915 hours and informed the units that the alarm had been an full scale exercise.

On that day the promotion of *Oberleutnant der Reserve* Hinzpeter to the rank of *Hauptmann der Reserve* was received.

On 20 December, *Hauptmann* Haen was given leave. In his absence the commander of the *3. Kompanie, Hauptmann* Fischer, became acting commander of *Panzer-Abteilung 103.*

On 21 December, by the division's order, *Leutnant* Bernd Röseler was sent to *Panzer-Ersatz und Ausbildungs-Abteilung 10* in Zinten.

On 24 December, *Oberleutnant* Johl was appointed as commander of the staff company.

On Christmas Eve at 1400 hours, orders received from the division stated that *Panzer-Abteilung 103* should submit its request for transport by rail to the transportation command in Rome without delay as its regrouping was imminent.

On 25 December at 0300 hours, the transportation command in Rome sent the transport registration document and the time of entrainment. Before noon, the first (operational) staff officer of the *3. Panzergrenadier-Division* informed the unit that they would be transported to the east coast that evening, where they would be held in the corps reserve of the *LXXVI. Panzerkorps.*

A total of three trains were at the unit's disposal for the transport. The order to relocate was received at noon. Elements of the force for which no room was available on the three trains had to move on wheels. However, an additional train was issued in the afternoon. Loading started only after nightfall, which had been delayed by several hours. At 1030 hours the first trainload rolled out from Monte Rotondo railway station on 26 December and arrived in Manopello near Chieti two days later, on 28 December, at 0900 hours. Detrainment of the troops was completed in one-and-a-half hours.

On 26 December, the acting commander of the unit, *Hauptmann* Fischer, drove forward by car to gather information at the staff of *LXXVI. Panzerkorps.* The reconnaissance platoon also set out on wheels so that they could organize a quartering area and direct the troops to it in good time.

The second transport, under command of *Leutnant* Spiegel, started entrainment on 26 December at 1330 hours and moved out of Monte Rotondo railway station at 1730 hours. Next day at 0720 hours the train arrived at Portorecanati where it was parked all day. Unluckily for the Germans, two Allied fighter-bomber aircraft attacked the train and the railway station station at 0750 hours. Three locomotives received severe hits but nobody from the personnel of *Panzer-Abteilung 103* was wounded nor was any damage incurred. At 1140 hours another air attack was launched: this time six fighter-bombers swept upon the transport

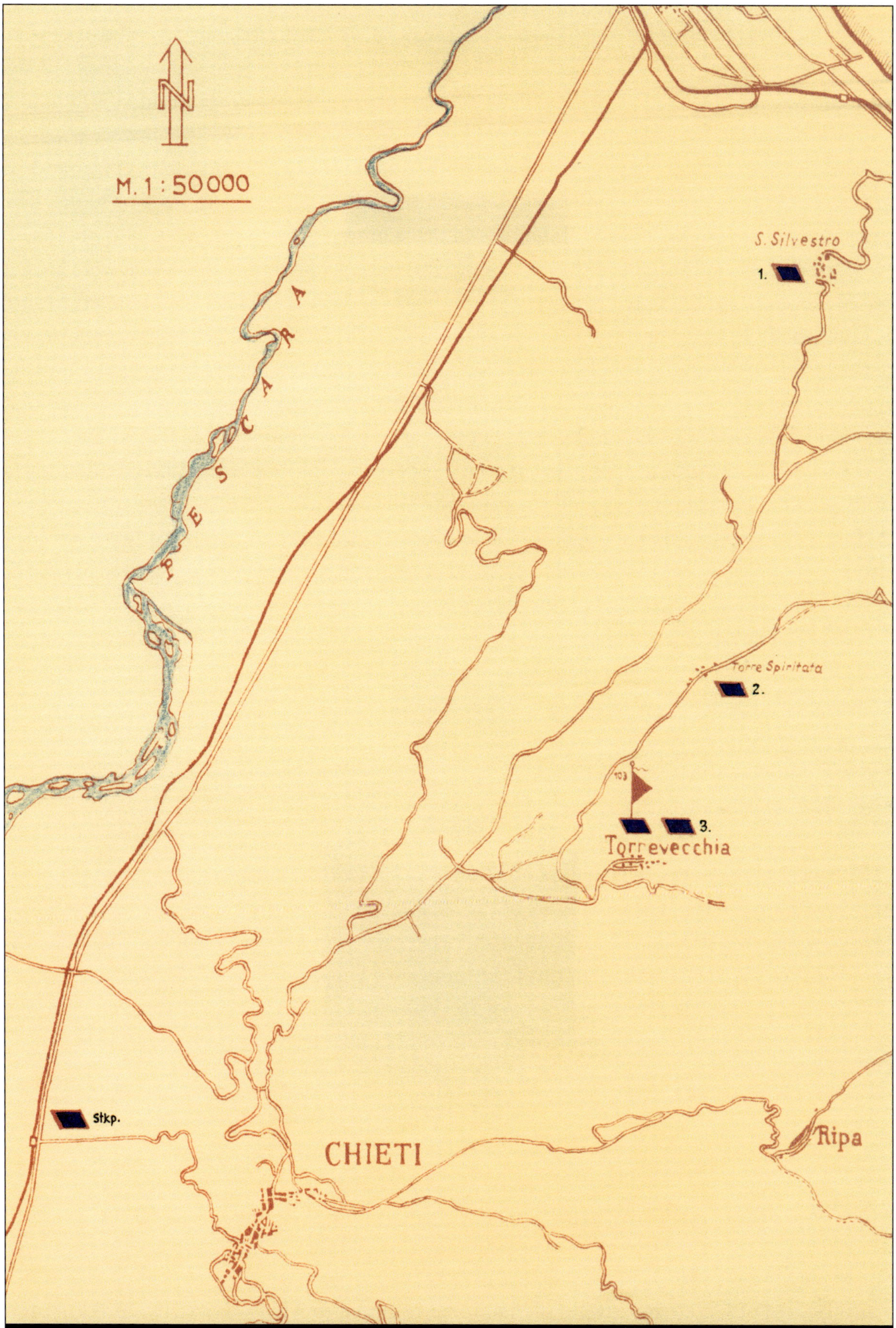

Quartering area of Panzer-Abteilung 103 on 28 December 1943

train which was divided into two parts. No casualties were suffered, but several trucks were hit and the one transporting fuel caught fire but the blaze was quickly extinguished. In the end, the transport arrived at Rosetto degli Abruzzi on 28 December, at around 0700 hours, and was detrained by 0815 hours.

The third train was loaded on 26 December at 2200 hours under the command of *Hauptmann der Reserve* Hinzpeter and departed the following morning at 0410 hours. The transport arrived at Chieti at 0730 hours and detrainment was completed at 0845 hours.

The fourth train transported the remaining wheeled vehicles of the unit which were loaded on 27 December at 0500 hours under the command of *Leutnant* Walz. The train left Monte Rotondo at 1730 hours and arrived at Senigallia on 28 December at 0800 hours, where it was parked until 1900 hours. At 1100 hours the railway station was raided from the air but the train was unharmed. At last, the transport arrived at Rosetto degli Abruzzi on 29 December, at 0630 hours, and was then unloaded – a process that was completed by 0815 hours.

The workshop platoon of the unit received orders to complete repairs already underway in its previous quartering area, and relocate only afterwards.

Part of the operational staff of *Panzer-Abteilung 103* under the command of *Leutnant* Kock also moved out on wheels from Oriolo on the afternoon of 27 December and arrived at Chieti, at the unit's temporary command post which was relocated on the same day to Torrevecchia.

Having completed the transportation process, the troops were in the following quartering areas:

- the staff company at the railway station of Chieti;
- the *1. Kompanie* in San Silvestro;
- the *2. Kompanie* in Torre Spiritata;
- the *3. Kompanie* in Torrevecchia.

The unit came under direct command of the *LXXVI. Panzerkorps* as corps reserve. Its supply was to be provided by the supply units of the *90. Panzergrenadier-Division.* Any maintenance needed was to be performed on armoured and wheeled vehicles by the repair and maintenance service of the *26. Panzer-Division* until the unit's own workshop platoon arrived.

Until the end of 1943, *Panzer-Abteilung 103* was not sent into action. Therefore the troops were able to spend their time improving their combat efficiency.

1944

In the area of Chieti any given task had to be confined to what was strictly necessary due to extremely intensive Allied air activity. *Hauptmann* Fischer and *Leutnant* Beschnidt were continuously surveying the area to find proper routes for assembly should an attack be ordered.

On 1 January, *Panzer-Abteilung 103* had 42 StuG. III assault guns (14 pieces per company), a command tank fitted with a long-barrelled 5cm gun and two others with short 5cm guns, a Panzer IB command tank and six 2cm towed AA guns.

On 5 January, *Leutnant* Recknagel relieved *Leutnant* Göb who supervised a maintenance detachment in Rome because the Germans had around 250 vehicles from the *3. Panzergrenadier-Division* undergoing repairs in the 25 civilian car-repair workshops in the Italian capital. The 200 men accompanying the vehicles were quartered in Hotel Universo. On the same day, *Leutnant* Göb was sent to *Feldersatz-Bataillon 3*, to which he was officially assigned as from 17 January.

On 6 January, *Leutnant* Kock became the acting commander of the 1st combat train *(Gefechtstroß I)*.

On 9 January, the workshop platoon of *Panzer-Abteilung 103* set off to follow its unit and, on the night of 9-10 January, it rolled into Tipurtina railway station in Rome on wheels, where the first half of the platoon entrained for transportation. However there were not enough wagons, so the remaining vehicles had to wait 8km from Rome under the leadership of engineer Günther. The entrained part of the unit left the Italian capital the same evening, but was delayed by demolished railroads halfway to its destination.

On 10 January, Allied fighter-bombers raided Torrevecchia. During the attack the command post of *Panzer-Abteilung 103* was destroyed. However, the casualties comprised of only two lightly wounded men. Some of the vehicles were slightly damaged. The new command post was set up on the same day, on the road running between Chieti and San Giovanni Teatino.

Hauptmann Heller was placed on the unattached list of the German Army with effect from the same day.

On 11 January, *Hauptmann* Fischer was awarded the German Cross in Gold for his achievements in Stalingrad and along the River Volturno.

On 12 January, *Leutnant* Walz was put in charge of building a supply road. For that purpose an Italian construction company of 280 men was put at his disposal. Trucks were provided by *Panzer-Abteilung 103* and tools and equipment were supplied by *Fallschirm-Pionier-Bataillon I.*

On that day the *1. Kompanie* was pulled out of its quartering area and subordinated to the paratrooper battalion of *Hauptmann* Heinz Schrader. The assault gun platoon, commanded by *Leutnant* Cramme took up position east of Tolle and was given the task to defend the main combat line in case of an armoured attack. Meanwhile, most of the company remained in Tolle. The sector was quiet so, until their relief on 20 January, the assault guns would not make contact with the Allies.

On 15 January, *Panzer-Abteilung 103* received an additional four assault guns, this time from *Panzer-Abteilung 190.* One was given to each of the *1. and 2. Kompanien*, two were issued to the *3. Kompanie.* Thus, as every company of the unit awaited further developments in Italy, they had been brought up to full strength of 14 assault guns in each company. However, the four newly arrived assault guns were in a dire technical condition and so were to be repaired before going into action by *Werkstatt-Kompanie 654* which was stationed in Chieti.

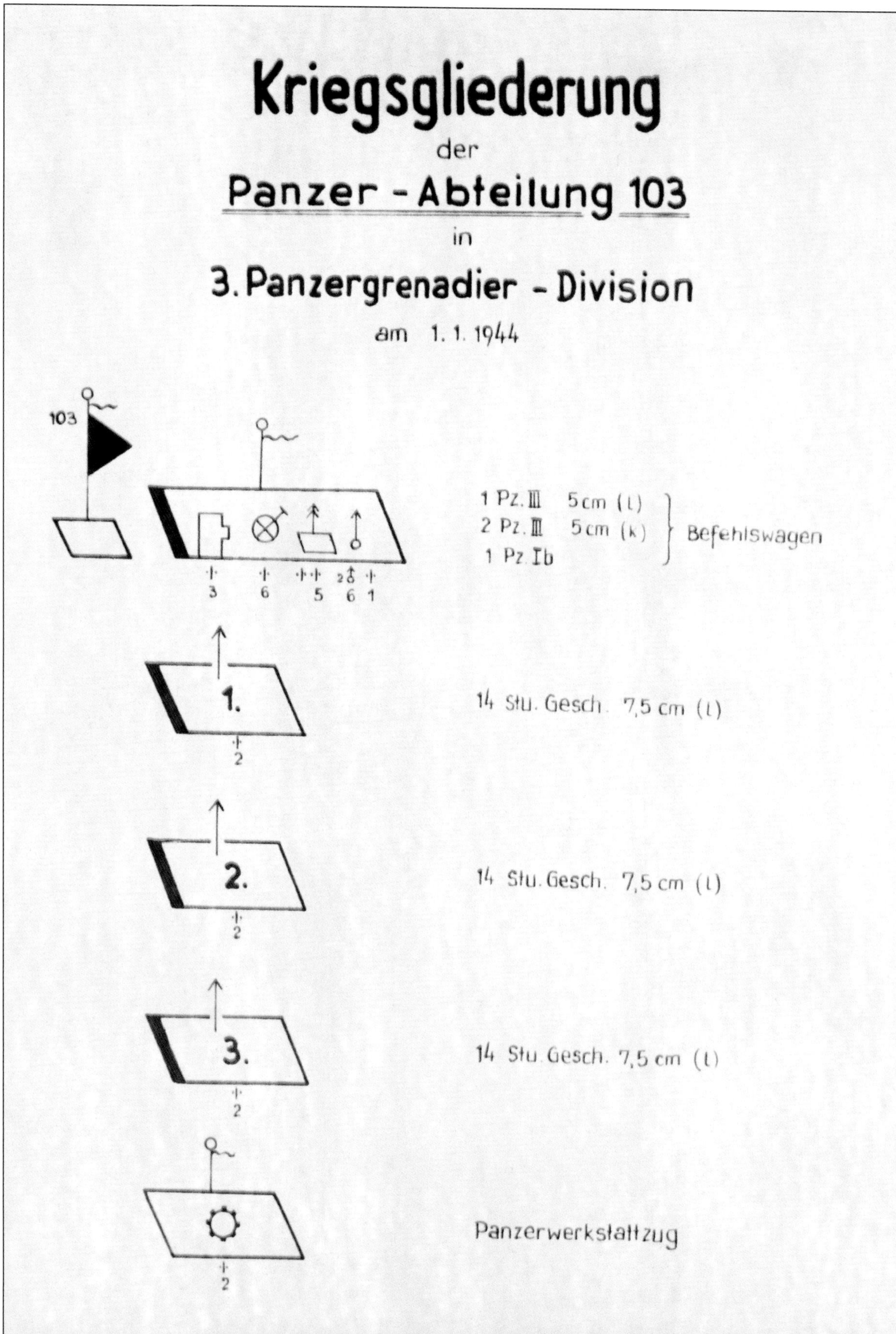

Order of battle of Panzer-Abteilung 103 on 1 January 1944

On 18 January, *Panzer-Abteilung 103* received orders from the staff of the *LXXVI. Panzerkorps* to regroup on the front line near Cassino in the area east-south-east of Sora. The unit immediately started to prepare for the movement and the following day each subunit also received the order to relocate. According to the plans, tracked vehicles were to be transported by three trains but wheeled vehicles were to reach the designated area unaided.

On that day *Leutnant* Walther arrived at the unit and took over the tasks of the orderly officer.

However, since Allied air raids had damaged railroads at several places, the next instruction issued on 19 January ordered the whole armoured unit to regroup 'on foot.'

On 20 January, each and every element of the unit was on its way. A temporary command post was established in Isola del Liri. The march through the icy and snow-covered passes proved to be an ordeal, especially for the tracked vehicles. Despite the continuous air raids carried out by the Allied fighter-bombers, the unit made progress in accordance with its plans owing to the undisturbed fuel supply and the commitment on the part of the repair and maintenance service. Of course, there were breakdowns during the march, especially among the tracked vehicles; due to the difficult terrain, engine and brake failures were unavoidable. However these problems were quickly overcome by the repair and maintenance and the recovery detachments. In the course of the march only one total loss occurred; in the area of Rocca di Mezzo Allied fighter-bombers set a fuel dump and a heavy truck on fire.

On 21 January, both parts of the unit's distant workshop platoon received orders from *Panzer-Abteilung 103* to march on wheels to the area of Isola del Liri. In the meantime, the first news of American and British landings in the area of Nettuno was received. Consequently, the workshop platoon was redirected, this time to the Olgiata manor near Via Cassia, 18km west of Rome.

5

Against the Anzio bridgehead in the area of Aprilia

On 22 January, the elements of *Panzer-Abteilung 103* were still on the march when, following the landing of American and British troops, the unit was practically turned around and sent back to the area of Frascati. During this march the Allied air activity, including fighter-bomber attacks, was completed by air raids conducted by larger bomber formations.

On 23 January, the unit's command post was in Zaragollo. *Hauptmann* Haen returned from his leave that day and immediately assumed command of *Panzer-Abteilung 103.* He relocated his command post to 3km south of Albano in the evening.

On 24 January, the unit was working at full blast to fix technical defects and improve their fighting capacity. As a result of their ceaseless work, most AFVs were made combat-ready.

On 25 January, one of the brigades of the British 1st Division,[97] with the support of a tank company of the 46th Royal Tank Regiment and two artillery regiments occupied Aprilia in a heavy fight. However, the hills 1km north of the settlement were successfully defended and the attack was halted by the *III. Bataillon* of *Grenadier-Regiment (mot.) 29.*[98]

In the afternoon *Panzer-Abteilung 103* carried out a reconnaissance attempt along the Albano–Nettuno highway during which they reached a point 500m north of Aprilia without establishing contact with the enemy. After nightfall, the *2. Kompanie* was given the task of securing the highway from a southerly direction. Meanwhile most of the unit returned to its quartering area.

At night *Panzer-Abteilung 103* received orders to provide support with eight Tiger heavy AFVs of armoured company *'Schwebbach'*[99] for the reconnaissance mission towards Aprilia which was conducted by *Grenadier-Regiment (mot.) 29.*[100] *Panzer-Abteilung 103* was given

---

97 According to records of 25 January 1944, a tank company of the British 46th Royal Tank Regiment fought in the area, supporting the 24th Guards Brigade of the British 1st Division. *See* Liddel Hart, B. H.: The Tanks. *The History of the Royal Tank Regiment. Volume Two,* 1939–1945. p. 277.

98 Dieckhoff, Gerhard: 3. Infanterie-Division – *3. Infanterie-Division (mot.) – 3. Panzergrenadier-Division* Cuxhaven, s.a., p. 289.

99 That independent heavy armoured company is generally known as *schwere Panzerkompanie 'Meyer'* in the literature. The reason for that must be the fact, that having its first commander, *Hauptmann* Hans Schwebbach killed in action on 26 January 1944, the command of the company was taken over by *Leutnant* Meyer. Based on the orders issued on 26 July 1943, it was established as an independent unit equipped with eight Tiger E heavy tanks, then it was merged into *schwere Panzer-Abteilung 508* on 3 March 1944. *See* Schneider, Wolfgang: *Tiger im Kampf. Band II.* p. 105.

100 Dieckhoff, Gerhard: *3. Infanterie-Division – 3. Infanterie-Division (mot.) – 3. Panzergrenadier-Division* Cuxhaven, s.a., p. 289. According to the information found on that page, the aim of the attack was not to carry out reconnaissance duty, but to retake Aprilia. British forces defending Aprilia was attacked by the armoured group swerving eastwards as well as by the *III. Bataillon* (reinforced with two pioneer platoons) of *Grenadier-Regiment (mot.) 29* pushing forward from a northerly direction.

the task of launching an attack the next day at dawn from its readiness position at Point 93 along the Albano–Nettuno highway, 2km south of the railway overpass, outflanking Aprilia from the right, and then pressing forward to the railroad and the highway south of the settlement.

On 26 January at dawn, the *3. Kompanie* was at the head of *Panzer-Abteilung 103*[101], followed by the staff of the unit, the *1. Kompanie*, the Tiger heavy AFVs and the assault guns of the *2. Kompanie* with grenadiers and a pioneer platoon riding on the top of them. The direction of the attack was as follows: the railway overpass by Point 93, down the highway towards south-west and across Points 105, 103 and 94.

Progress was good across Points 105 and 103. The *3. Kompanie* moved across Point 94 on the highway in a south-westerly direction up to Point 74 and then turned towards south-east to follow the railway embankment in a hollow in the direction of Stazione di Aprilia (the railway station of that settlement).

The *1. Kompanie* and the Tiger heavy tanks deployed east of the highway then opened fire on British Sherman III tanks and AT guns that had been identified in the area of Aprilia and Stazione di Aprilia.

However, German fortunes soon changed. They were unable to press home their attack due to the terrain which was disadvantageous for the armoured combat vehicles and, in the midst of Allied tank, AT and artillery fire, they were sustaining increasing losses.

When the Allied fire became heavier, *Hauptmann* Haen decided to send the *1. Kompanie* through the hollow together with the Tiger heavy tanks to reinforce the *3. Kompanie*. By so doing, he shifted the focal point of the attack towards Stazione di Aprilia.

The *3. Kompanie* was able to advance only a short distance along the railway embankment towards south-east, before it was halted by the adverse ground conditions and the Allied fire. The Tiger tanks were stuck in the muddy terrain and could not go further. During the engagement, the assault gun of *Oberfähnrich* Grafe destroyed an Allied AFV, an AT gun, two trucks and one car, and took 30 POWs. On the other hand two assault guns of the *3. Kompanie* received severe hits: one of them was burnt out, the other was immobilized. Since a recovery attempt failed under enemy fire and the main combat line was to be pulled back during the night by orders of the *3. Panzergrenadier-Division,* the immobilized StuG. III was blown up by *Leutnant* Zaunmüller following the orders he had received.

Meanwhile the assault guns of the *2. Kompanie*, with the grenadiers riding on the top of them, closed up by orders of *Hauptmann* Haen and they too came under Allied artillery and AT fire. One of the StuG. III assault guns received five hits and totally burnt out. A hit by an AT shell tore away one of the tracks of another assault gun. However, after great difficulties, that AFV was successfully towed away later. The grenadiers were forced to get off the AFVs in the enemy fire and run for cover west of the highway.

At around 1200 hours the assault gun platoon of *Leutnant* Sippell was put under the direct command of *Grenadier-Regiment (mot.) 29,* which had commenced an attack from a northerly

---

101 Dieckhoff, Gerhard: *3. Infanterie-Division – 3. Infanterie-Division (mot.) – 3. Panzergrenadier-Division* Cuxhaven, s.a. On page 289 we read that elements of *II./ Panzer-Regiment 26* were also assigned to the battle group. However, it is not mentioned in the war diary of *Panzer-Abteilung 103.*

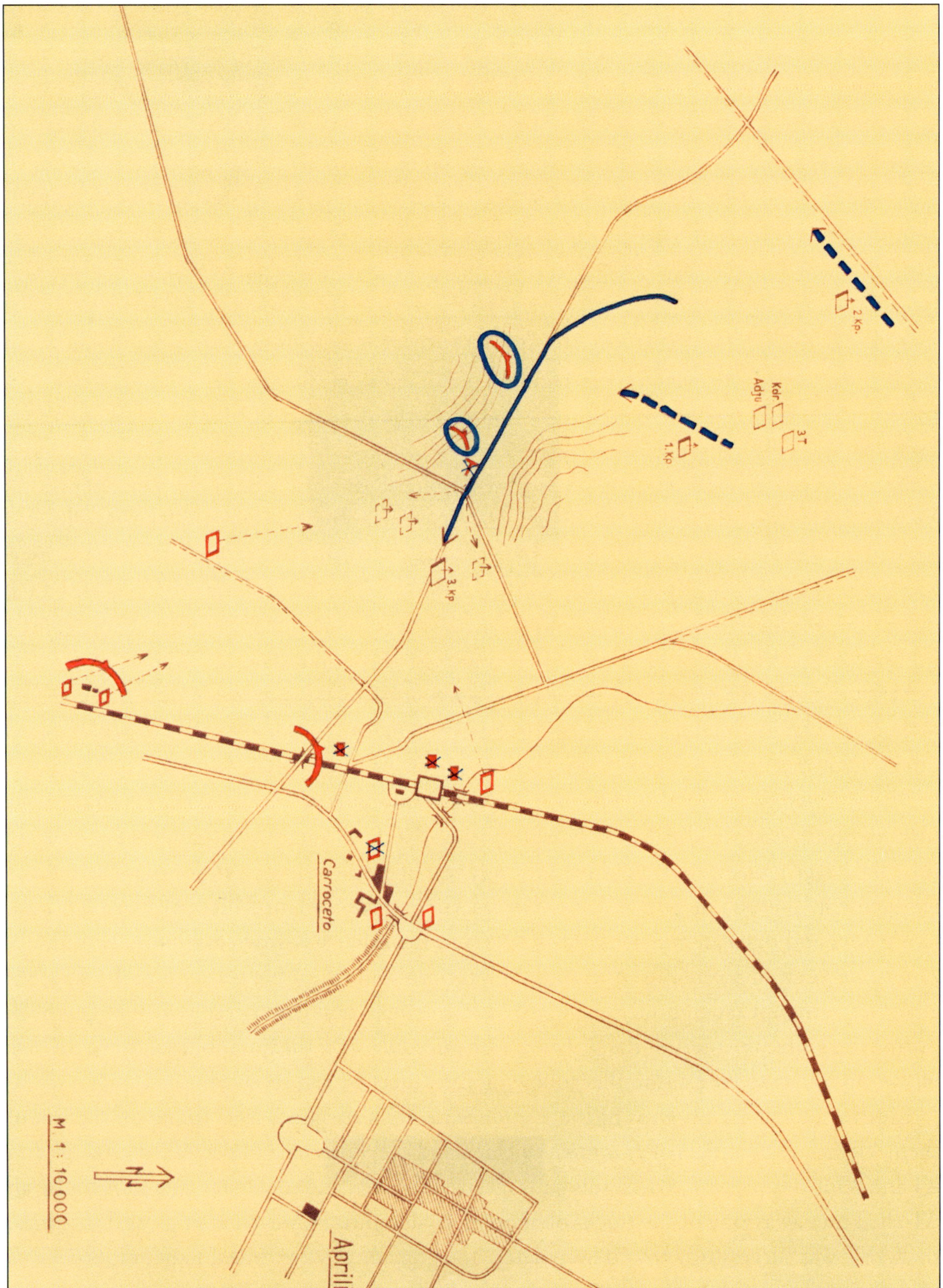

Situation map, 26 January 1944

direction towards Aprilia. One of the StuG. III assault guns of the platoon supporting the infantry suffered damage from enemy fire during the fighting.

Elements of *Grenadier-Regiment (mot.) 29* penetrated Aprilia from an easterly direction to the center of the settlement, but retreated from the town the same evening.[102]

The commander of the Tiger company, *Hauptmann* Schwebbach, was killed in the battle; *Leutnant* Gran of the *1. Kompanie* was seriously wounded from shell fragments. The German attack had no chance of success against the Allied artillery and AT fire. Despite that, *Panzer-Abteilung 103* and its subordinated Tiger company remained in their achieved positions until nightfall. Afterwards, the AFVs were withdrawn to the road junction at Point 135. The assault gun platoon *'Sippell'* continued to support *Grenadier-Regiment (mot.) 29.*

At 2300 hours orders were issued according to which *Panzer-Abteilung 103* was to return to its original readiness position south of Albano. That was carried out by the AFVs before sunrise. The recovery was led by *Leutnant* Beschnidt and, despite the difficulties presented by the constant Allied fire and difficult terrain, the Germans succeeded.

According to the war diary of *Panzer-Abteilung 103*, the main reason for the failure of the attack in which serious losses were sustained was – besides the terrain which was almost unpassable for the AFVs – the lack of artillery support. This is all the more inexplicable because the cooperation of the German artillery had been explicitly requested by the superior command.[103]

The balance of losses during the attack, which proved to be something of a fiasco for the Germans, was as follows:

- Allied losses: three Sherman tanks and four AT guns knocked out, another three Sherman tanks damaged, 30 POWs
- losses of the reinforced *Panzer-Abteilung 103*: three dead, four wounded, three StuG. IIIs written off as total losses, an additional five assault guns in need of repair.[104]

On the same day the pioneer platoon of *Panzer-Abteilung 103* was detached and put under the command of *Pionier-Bataillon (mot.) 3* by orders of the divisional command.

On 27 January the maintenance personnel played a major role in the day's events at the unit. Despite the continuous attacks carried out by the Allied fighter-bomber aircraft, they managed to get most of the damaged AFVs into combat-ready condition in a very short while.

At night assault gun platoon *'Sippell'*, subordinated to *Grenadier-Regiment (mot.) 29* to carry out securing tasks, was relieved by *Oberleutnant* Häusser with five assault guns of the *2. Kompanie*.

On 28 January, the command post of *Panzer-Abteilung 103* was relocated to 3km north-west of Cecchina. The three assault gun companies were employed in securing positions along the Rome–Cisterna railroad, separated from each other.

---

102 NARA T312, R483 (*Armeeoberkommando 14*), F8074821.

103 *Kriegstagebuch der Panzer-Abteilung 103* (copy in author's possession), p. 67.

104 *Kriegstagebuch der Panzer-Abteilung 103* (copy in author's possession), p. 67.

At night the assault guns of *Oberleutnant* Häusser, put into action in an advanced position with the grenadiers, were relieved by *Hauptmann der Reserve* Hinzpeter with the AFVs of the *1. Kompanie*.

On 29 January at dawn the StuG. III assault guns of the *2. Kompanie*, participated in a reconnaissance mission against a group of houses as of 0030 hours.

During the day the assault guns of *Panzer-Abteilung 103* were still involved in securing the front line. The Allies sent out some infantry reconnaissance patrols that were repulsed by the AFVs. The German positions were continuously attacked by significant artillery fire and fighter-bomber aircraft.

Because the Allies often used smoke-screens to conceal their troop assembly areas, the forward-deployed German assault guns received orders to fire into those smoke-screens regardless of restrictions on ammunition expenditure.

In the afternoon *Hauptmann der Reserve* Hinzpeter reported intensive Allied reconnaissance activity in front of the German positions. The German heavy weapons placed identified Allied assembly areas under fire. The assault guns of *Panzer-Abteilung 103* took a hand in the battle by acting as artillery.

During the day *Hauptmann* Haen was summoned by the division's commander to the command post, where it was announced that the commander of *Panzer-Abteilung 103* had been promoted to the rank of *Major.*

On the night from 29 to 30 January, Allied troops assembling in the bridgehead launched an attack on the sector of the *3. Panzergrenadier-Division.* On the left flank, at the positions held by battle group *'Schönfeld'* the attackers breached the German front line. At sunrise the infantry of the division commenced a counterthrust with the support of the assault guns of *Panzer-Abteilung 103* and the Hornisse heavy tank destroyers of *schwere Panzerjäger-Abteilung 525.* In the course of the battle the Allies knocked out two German heavy tank destroyers.

At around 0500 hours it became obvious to the Germans that their continuous main combat line had ceased to exist and that the British penetrated their positions. In spite of that, the Germans continued to put up resistance at certain points. So did the group of *Leutnant* Semrau made up of 18 soldiers gathered up from the *I. Bataillon* of *Grenadier-Regiment (mot.) 29,* remainders of an assault detachment, two StuG. III assault guns (probably from *Panzer-Abteilung 103*) and a Hornisse tank destroyer. The small battle group tried to contain the attackers until the German forces were able to withdraw to rear positions. During this delaying combat, the second lieutenant and his improvised battle group retook Hill 93 2km south of Campoleone, although they suffered severe losses during the engagement. They successfully held the hill against the attack launched by two British companies and 10 AFVs. At the end of the battle, which had been raging for hours, the British decided to bypass the Germans from the east. The resistance put up by the small battle group enabled *Grenadier-Regiment (mot.) 29* to establish a new front line farther back along the railway embankment.[105]

---

105 The second lieutenant was awarded the Knight's Cross of the German Iron Cross for his achievements. Dieckhoff, Gerhard: *3. Infanterie-Division – 3. Infanterie-Division (mot.) – 3. Panzergrenadier-Division* Cuxhaven, s.a., pp. 290-291.

Afterwards, the assault guns were mainly used for securing tasks against Allied combat vehicles. During that, the *2. Kompanie* knocked out two Allied tanks, the *3. Kompanie* destroyed an additional one, and the assault gun of *Oberfähnrich* Grafe heavily damaged a fourth enemy AFV. The *3. Sturmgeschütz-Kompanie* lost one dead and one soldier was seriously wounded by artillery fire during the battle. None of the assault guns were written off as a total loss.

Putting additional forces into action, the Allied troops broke through the German defences along the Aprilia–Albano highway during the day and approached the Rome–Cisterna railroad within 500m from a southerly direction. As a result, the securing assault guns of *Panzer-Abteilung 103* were withdrawn during the night to the northern side of the railway embankment.

On 31 January in the morning, the British infantry – normally in battalion-size groups – jumped off along the whole of the front line and in the area of Stazione di Campoleone they managed to penetrate the German positions in depth with the support of the AFVs of the 46th Royal Tank Regiment.

The main task of the British was to reach the road fork near Osteriaccia and eliminate German positions along the railway embankment which would then make it possible for the US 1st Armored Division to put its forces into action to achieve a breakthrough.

The British troops were somehow able to struggle across the railway embankment but they were halted there. The violent fire of the German defenders – complemented by the fire of the assault guns of *Panzer-Abteilung 103* acting as artillery – not only halted the attack, but also forced the British infantry to retreat. Some of the StuG. III assault guns broke into buildings from behind to shell the British through the windows.[106]

On that day from 1200 hours, the *715. Infanterie-Division* and the artillery units of *Arko 122* came under command of the *3. Panzergrenadier-Division,* and by so doing, group *'Gräser'* was formed.

At 1540 hours Germans observed another Allied armoured and infantry concentration[107] 500m south of Stazione di Campoleone. Several StuG. III assault guns took firing positions 250m from the railroad. The Germans placed the assembly area under fire and quickly repulsed the unfolding Allied attack.

However, the attackers didn't give up the fight easily and made an additional four attempts, all of which were repelled by the Germans. The fighting ceased at around 1800 hours, by which time the Germans had steadfastly held their main combat line.

During the day's fighting the assault guns of *Panzer-Abteilung 103* stabilized the German infantry defence several times and therefore made a significant contribution to the success of the defence. Besides fighting against enemy armour, the assault gun companies had to provide artillery support for their own infantry and intercept or disperse enemy infantry. On that day the StuG. III assault guns of the unit knocked out a total of four Allied tanks and damaged one more. One of the tanks had struck a mine and was totally destroyed by *Leutnant* Cramme in close combat.

---

106 Dieckhoff, Gerhard: *3. Infanterie-Division – 3. Infanterie-Division (mot.) – 3. Panzergrenadier-Division* Cuxhaven, s.a., p. 291.

107 Those were probably elements of the US 1st Armored Division. *See* Dieckhoff, Gerhard: *3. Infanterie-Division – 3. Infanterie-Division (mot.) – 3. Panzergrenadier-Division* Cuxhaven, s.a., p. 291.

The personnel of *Panzer-Abteilung 103* were unable to rest even at the end of the day because the Allies had sent reconnaissance patrols into action one after another and their artillery also remained active throughout the night.

Hauptmann Fischer departed on leave. Command of the 3. Sturmgeschütz-Kompanie was taken over by *Leutnant* Zaunmüller.

On 1 February before noon, soldiers of *Panzer-Abteilung 103* observed Allied forces digging in 800m south of the Rome–Cisterna railroad.

At 1200 hours the Allied infantry was preparing to launch an attack along the Albano–Nettuno railway and highway. Having informed their artillery immediately, the Germans placed the assembly area under fire and by destroying it nipped the attack in the bud.

During the battles fought during the previous two days, the Allies suffered heavy casualties and as a result of this they temporarily gave up further attacks. Their fighting activity was limited mainly to artillery actions complemented by fire from naval guns targeting the German positions and supply routes. However, Allied bomber and fighter-bomber activity was increased. The Germans were also harassed by the intensive activity of reconnaissance patrols and assault squads.

Certain elements of *Panzer-Abteilung 103* continued to secure behind the front line but, at the same time, intensive maintenance was performed on all battle-worn assault guns. The prime mover platoon and the repair detachments worked day and night, as did the supply subunit.

According to the figures of the same day, the German *14. Armee* possessed the following combat-ready armoured forces in the area (without the AFVs involved in the coastal defences):

- 11 Panzer IV tanks (long-barrelled)
- five flamethrower tanks
- four Tiger E heavy tanks
- seven German command tanks (including the AFVs of *Panzer-Abteilung 103*)
- three Italian-made command tanks
- 22 German assault guns (including the AFVs of *Panzer-Abteilung 103*)
- 26 Italian-made assault guns.[108]

On 2 February, during the noon hours, the Allied artillery fire was intensified. Then, under cover of the sound of the heavy weapons, the Allied troops infiltrated forward in the area of Stazione di Campoleone. However, the Germans repulsed them.

At 1430 hours a report was received by *Panzer-Abteilung 103,* about 72 Allied AFVs assembling east of the highway running to Nettuno. At the same time, smoke and phosphorus shells were poured onto the German positions by the Allied artillery. At around 1900 hours the attack intensified into a barrage, but after another 50 minutes the Allied weapons suddenly ceased fire.

On 3 February during the day, the tactical situation was the same. Therefore *Panzer-Abteilung 103* received orders from group *'Gräser'* in the evening to launch an attack north of

108 The German Operation at Anzio. Produced at GMDS by a combined British, Canadian and U.S. Staff, 1946., p. 33.

Aprilia to eliminate the Allied troops that had broken through and to reoccupy the original main combat line.

The attack of the battle group *'Gräser'* was joined on the right flank by the *65. Infanterie-Division.* The sector to be taken back extended from Point 64, 4km west of Aprilia to Point 80, 2km north-west of that settlement.

In relation to that, the commander of the German *14. Armee, Generaloberst* Eberhard von Mackensen, issued the following order:

'An attack is imperative. Under all circumstances constant blows against the enemy, at least with strong assault detachments, must be delivered along the entire front. This will give us intelligence of the enemy situation, and the enemy, expecting an attack, will be forced to disperse his troops. Partial blows in preparation for the decisive offensive aiming to wipe out the beachhead should be delivered with all available forces in order to weaken the enemy.

Therefore, I order:

First, the elimination of the enemy in the penetrated sector north of Aprilia, as planned by the Headquarters of I. Fallschirm-Korps *for the night of 3 to 4 February 1944.*

Second, that the present main line of resistance be held in the sectors which are not in active combat at the moment. Assault detachments will attack the enemy continuously. Our forces will be shifted in accordance with enemy moves.

Forces will be reduced rapidly in sectors where the enemy is inactive.

In order to destroy the enemy near Aprilia this detailed plan will take effect: 'Western Group" will push forward in an easterly direction from the area north and south of Hill 102.

The 'Eastern Group' will fight in a westerly direction toward the railroad from the area 1km south of Cle. della Mandria. Then, after establishing a defence line in the south, the enemy should be up in a northern direction.

'Western Group' will consist of a reinforced Grenadier-Regiment 145 *of the* 65. Infanterie Division, *three infantry battalions, two light artillery battalions, and two combat engineer companies. It will be equipped with ten 8.8cm self-propelled guns (Hornisse), and three heavy anti-tank guns.*

The 'Eastern Group', will comprise of a reinforced Panzergrenadier-Regiment 104, *two light artillery battalions, three infantry battalions, and two combat engineer companies. It will be equipped with 8 (Hornisse) and 4 heavy anti-tank guns. There is a reserve of 12 assault guns, in addition to the detached 'Artillery Group' with three light artillery battalions, nine heavy artillery battalions, including mortars and 17cm guns, and rocket launchers.*

Should the outcome of this attack be favourable, strong assault detachments will push southwards, past the planned main line of resistance, to seize the enemy stronghold at the road junction 1.5km north of Aprilia.

Outposts will be established there. The artillery, the anti-aircraft artillery, and the combat engineers, are assigned to support.

Combat Group 'Gräser', *will be brought forward immediately, after the completion of the operation. This will enable us to follow up our attack, during the night of 4 to 5 February 1944, and to capture Aprilia. For the attack the* I. Abteilung *of* Panzer-Regiment 4, *equipped with Panther tanks, will be attached to the* LXXVI. Panzerkorps. *However, tanks and assault guns will attack with the infantry; they will not precede the infantry."*[109]

Thus, to carry out the attack, group *'Gräser'* put two battle groups into action: the reinforced *Grenadier-Regiment 145,* commanded by colonel Kühl, and the reinforced *Panzergrenadier-Regiment 104* of colonel Ens[110].

Battle group *'Kühl'* was given the task to advance eastwards from the south-eastern foreground of Panichi up to the Stazione di Campoleone–Nettuno railroad. Battle group *'Ens'* also started its drive towards there from the south-western foreground of Colle della Mandria.

Having reached the railroad and joined forces, the two battle groups were supposed to eliminate the Allied troops by launching an attack northwards. Having completed that, they were to establish defensive positions along the general line of Point 68 – Point 63 – the railway and road junction 50m north-east of it – Point 82 – Point 79, and securing southwards to repel every attack.

The focal point of the German attack was in the sector held by battle group *'Ens'*. The Allied troops, having taken up position across the railway embankment, were contained from 2400 hours by the Germans who feigned preparation for an attack there as of 2400 hours. *Panzer-Abteilung 103,* reinforced with Tiger heavy tanks would have been brought forward after mopping up the cauldron and the routes running southwards from the previous main combat line, because significant Allied armoured force might have been trapped in the encirclement.

At the time of delivering the order to attack, the assault gun companies were still in securing positions along the Rome–Cisterna–Littoria railroad, and remained there until sunrise, in accordance with the orders received.

On 4 February at 0600 hours, *Major* Haen was summoned to the divisional command post because the German infantry had reported that its forces reached the area of Point 95 and had secured it from a southerly direction. Following that, *Panzer-Abteilung 103* received orders to reach the area of Point 95 together with the attached Tiger company, following the route of Point 103–Point 93–Point 80. The Tiger heavy tanks moved at the head of the marching column, followed by the staff of *Panzer-Abteilung* and the assault guns of the *2.*, the *1.* and the *3. Kompanie.*

During the march the lead Tiger heavy tank of *Leutnant* Meyer was hit front-wise by an Allied AT gun, and had to be towed away to the rear across Point 93. The heavy tank following fought down the AT gun and the advance continued.

The *1. Kompanie* of *Panzer-Abteilung 103,* under the command of *Hauptmann der Reserve* Hinzpeter, and reinforced by three Tigers, received orders to reach the Albano–Aprilia highway across Point 95.

While crossing Point 95, the second Tiger heavy tank in the column was hit from the right by an AT gun and totally burnt out. After that, the Tiger of *Leutnant* Euen, which had

109 The German Operation at Anzio. Produced at GMDS by a combined British, Canadian and U.S. Staff, 1946., pp. 29-30.

110 The former regiment belonged to the order of battle of the *65. Infanterie-Division*, and the latter to that of the *15. Panzergrenadier-Division*.

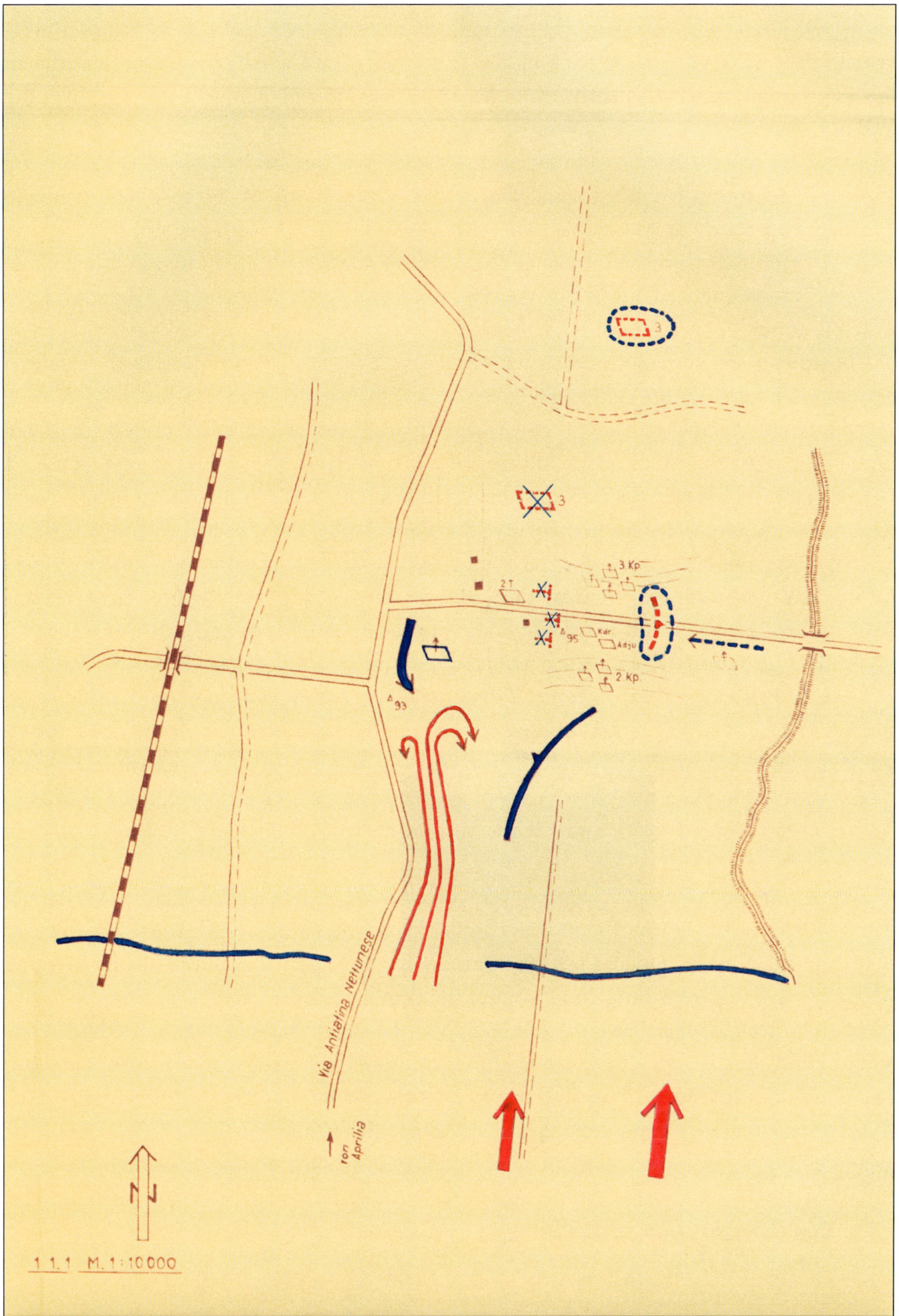

Situation map, 4 February 1944

passed the Point unharmed and was just rolling downhill, opened fire at an Allied combat vehicle and an AT gun giving flanking fire from the right. The Allied AFV was destroyed, but the AT gun, in its excellently camouflaged position put up behind a slope, didn't offer a good target yet.

That AT gun knocked out and burnt down another Tiger heavy tank on the drive. Yet another heavy combat vehicle became bogged down 200m north of Point 95 while trying to bypass it from north. It was unable to move unaided.

It was then that the assault guns of the *1. Kompanie* were drawn forward, but four of them were soon knocked out by the Allied AT guns and AFVs. Three StuG. III assault guns were burnt out.

Those heavy armoured losses occurred as a result of the false report made by the infantry, because – contrary to the statements given – thc area around Point 95 had not yet been cleared by the grenadiers. The AT gun which knocked out the lead Tiger heavy tank had been observed by the AFVs, but in full awareness of the report mentioned, they took it for a German gun.[111] However, this does still not explain why the assault guns were brought forward without sufficient protection, particularly after the Tiger heavy tanks had been disabled.

In the emerging situation *Major* Haen immediately required infantry and artillery support for his AFVs, especially to eliminate the Allied AT guns giving flanking fire. The Germans gave up their intention to bypass Point 95 due to the impassable terrain.

While waiting for the support to arrive, the assault guns of *Panzer-Abteilung 103,* still combat-ready, secured Point 95 from all directions: the *2. Kompanie* took up position along the hill in a southerly direction facing the road running to Nettuno, with the *3. Kompanie* on the highway at Point 93 northwards. The recovery of the bogged-down Tiger heavy tank failed for now, although two other Tigers plus the command tank of the adjutant of *Panzer-Abteilung 103* tried to tow it away. It was successfully pulled out only after nightfall by a prime mover sent there.

The assault guns of the *1. Kompanie* were forced to repel the ceaseless attacks of a Ranger battalion without any infantry support and under the heaviest artillery fire. Those attacks failed again and again in the gun and machine-gun fire of the StuG. III assault guns. By nightfall 75 Allied dead had been counted in front of the company's positions.

At 1445 hours, *Major* Haen reported that his AFVs had knocked out three Allied tanks and three AT guns that day. The German losses amounted to three Tiger heavy tanks and five assault guns, including the Tiger and three StuG. III assault guns that had been destroyed.

According to the figures reported the same evening, the German *14. Armee* had the following armoured forces in the area (without combat vehicles involved in the costal defence):

- 20 Panzer IV tanks (long-barrelled)
- 59 Panther tanks
- six flamethrower tanks

111 *Kriegstagebuch der Panzer-Abteilung 103* (copy in author's possession), p. 75.

- zero Tiger E heavy tanks
- seven German command tanks
- six Italian command tanks
- 18 German assault guns
- 29 Italian assault guns.[112]

After nightfall the job of recovering the assault guns of *Panzer-Abteilung 103* was sped up despite having no artillery support whatsoever and the fact that the Allied artillerymen had no intention of retiring for the night.

On 5 February at 0700 hours, *Panzer-Abteilung 103* started off southwards down the highway but, at the same time, they left a detachment behind to secure northwards.

At 0743 hours *Major* Haen reported to the commander of group *'Gräser'*, that the area of the encircled troops had been combed along the main route, but was found to be almost empty.[113]

Afterwards, in the remaining part of the day, the assault guns of the unit performed security duties along the highway, at Point 93, despite the ever-present Allied artillery fire.

At sunset two assault guns of the *3. Kompanie* (their commanders: *Leutnant* Zaunmüller and *Oberfähnrich* Grafe) performed security duty west of Point 89 while the most of the other two companies did the same under the command of *Leutnant* Spengler[114] at Point 95, on the highway from a southerly direction.

On 6 February, the situation was the same. *Panzer-Abteilung 103* was still holding its securing positions while under severe Allied artillery fire and constant attacks by bombers. Moreover, the Allies launched several reconnaissance and assault attempts which all proved ineffective.

Apart from a few wounded, the German armoured unit suffered no losses.

On 7 February, *Panzer-Abteilung 103* received orders to commence yet another attack. The *2. Kompanie*, in the area of Point 95, prepared to support the attack of battle group *'Schönfeld'* to retake Aprilia, while the *1.* and the *3. Kompanie* made ready to provide support south of Point 118. Following the infantry's successful night attack, the armoured forces would have been put into action against the settlement only at dawn, in close cooperation with the infantry. Having occupied Aprilia, the assault guns were to prepare to beat off Allied armour. The order for this, issued by *Major* Haen, was drafted as follows:

'[…]

1. The enemy:

The much-weakened British 1. [Infantry-] *Division that had lost about 50% of its infantry was relieved by the British 56th Infantry division*[115] *on the 6th and on the night from the 6th to the 7th of February. Weak securing strongpoints along the line of Point 64–Point 71–Guardapassi–*

112 The German Operation at Anzio. Produced at GMDS by a combined British, Canadian and U.S. Staff, 1946., p. 33.

113 During the day the commander of the reconnaissance platoon, *Leutnant* Beschnidt fetched five ammunition carriers, an American mortar with ammunition, a German medium mortar, two British motorcycles and a British truck from the area of the encirclement for the unit.

114 In the day's fighting *Oberleutnant Häusser* was wounded in the head by shell fragments and was taken to hospital. Due to that, command of the *2. Kompanie* was taken over by *Leutnant* Spengler.

115 As a matter of fact, only the 168th Infantry Brigade of that British division arrived as reinforcement, and relived the decimated 3rd Infantry Brigade of the 1st Division. *See* Zaloga, Steven J.: Anzio 1944. Campaign 155, Osprey Publishing. Oxford, 2005. p. 49.

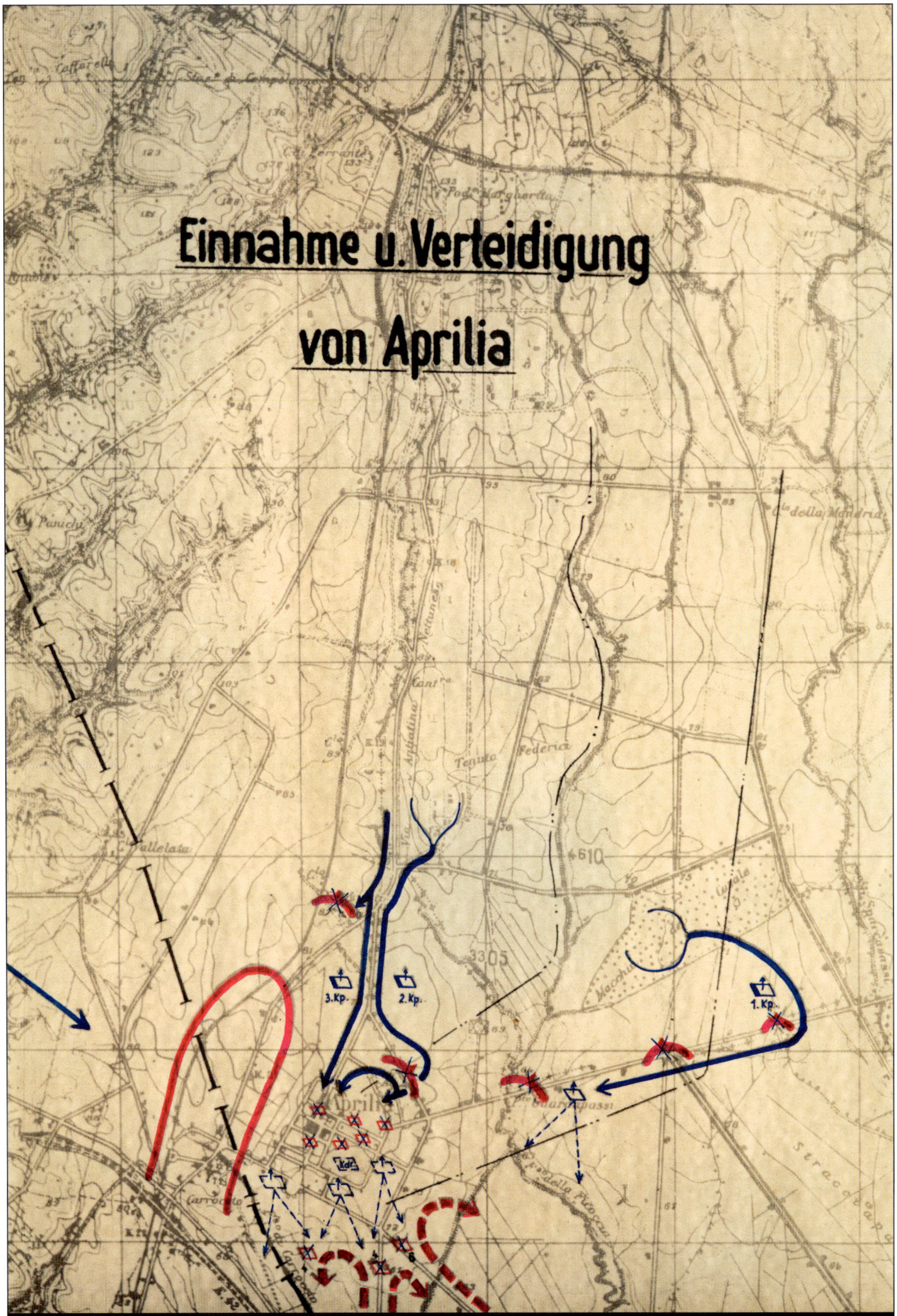

Situation map, 7-9 February 1944

Barracks–Point 78–Point 81 were significantly reinforced on the night from the 6th to the 7th of February, therefore the reconnaissance in force against Aprilia could not be carried out. Strongpoint 'Spider'*, the bridge 1km east of it and the towel-shaped small forest were occupied by our own forces. Enemy armour*[116] *(two or three AFVs) was identified in their camouflaged defensive positions 800m north of Aprilia, at Point 81.*

2. Battle group 'Gräser' *occupies Aprilia by a night attack, launched from an easterly direction, as its focal point. To relieve enemy pressure against the attacking forces, the 65.* Infanterie-Division *makes rapid progress towards Stazione Carroceto and takes it.*

3. The execution of the attack:

A reinforced battalion of Grenadier-Regiment 104 *commences an attack at 2030 hours down the Aprilia–Point 64–Point 71 route, breaches these positions and rolls them up in an easterly direction. It is followed closely by* Grenadier-Regiment 29 *from right and* Grenadier-Regiment 735 *from left, both pressing through the breaching point and, for the time being only* Grenadier-Regiment 29 *takes the trench in the area of F. della Ficoccia, while* Grenadier-Regiment 735 *occupies the designated main combat line about one, 1-1,5 kilometres from the highway.*

The second phase of the attack is initiated by annihilating artillery fire on Aprilia and on the positions east of the settlement. Exploiting the artillery fire, Grenadier-Regiment 29 *attacks and takes Aprilia, then links up with the* 65. Infanterie-Division *and occupies the designated main combat line south of Aprilia.*

In order to further relieve the pressure on the attack, elements of the 715. Infanterie-Division *start off from a northerly direction (from the area of* [strongpoint], 'Spider'*) towards Aprilia with the special task of containing the enemy forces there.*

4. The task of Panzer-Abteilung 103 *is to support the grenadiers in combat from sunrise, and to provide anti-tank defence immediately in the new main combat line. In accordance with that*

- *the 1. and the 3. Kompanien prepare themselves at the Mandria road fork with their lead AFVs 1km south of the railway crossover*
- *the 2. Kompanie prepares itself in the area of Point 96.*

The unit's command post is at the command post of Grenadier-Regiment 29 *north of Mandria, then at Point 70, on the north-western perimeter of the towel-shaped small forest.*

5. The tasks of the individual companies:

- *The 1. and the 3. Kompanien are to be ready to take up position in the towel-shaped forest in accordance with orders received by radio, and to be able to start off down the road from Point 64 towards Aprilia.*

116 The British 1st (Infantry-) Division was still supported at that time by the 46th Royal Tank Regiment – a unit of battalion size, equipped with Sherman tanks.

- *The 2. Kompanie at Point 95 remains at its commander's disposal, with its positions towards south, but prepares itself to be able either to support the fight of the grenadiers moving out through Mandria or in a southerly direction, or to be included in the antitank defence of the new main combat line.*

6. The supply of the Abteilung *has to be completed by 2000 hours on 7 February, 1944 at the latest. The 1. and the 3. Kompanie have to take up their jump-off positions by 2100 hours. [...]*'[117]

By 2100 hours the *2. Kompanie* of *Panzer-Abteilung 103* was put on readiness at Point 95, with the *1. and the 3. Kompanien* on standby for action south of Point 118 to support battle group *'Schönfeld'*. Apart from providing support for the infantry assault on Aprilia, the assault guns were to take over the task of securing against enemy armour at the bridge called Ponte Guardapassi south of Road 64.

By the morning of 8 February the attack of the grenadiers – especially the *II. and the III. Bataillone* of *Grenadier-Regiment (mot.) 29* – initially progressed according to plan. However, the *II. Bataillon* of the regiment was halted south of Road 64 mainly due to the flanking fire from the road crossing at Point 71. However, *Grenadier-Regiment 735* started off from the southern foreground of Mandria only three hours later, while the *III. Bataillon* of *Grenadier-Regiment (mot.) 29* had occupied the barracks and the cemetery at around midnight by surprise. The Allies launched a counterthrust from Aprilia towards the cemetery and the barracks with the support of five combat vehicles, forcing the *III. Bataillon* of *Grenadier-Regiment (mot.) 29* to withdraw to the trench of Fosso della Ficoccia with its front line to the west.

The night attack launched by the German infantry was soon halted but, at dawn, they were supposed to have resumed their attack together with the assault guns of *Panzer-Abteilung 103*. To this end, the *1. Kompanie* was brought forward to the towel-shaped small forest, and the *2. Kompanie* to *Stütztpunk 'Spinne'* (strongpoint 'Spider'). Nevertheless, the Germans did not continue their attack that day, because the *II. Bataillon* of *Grenadier-Regiment (mot.) 29* and the forces of *Grenadier-Regiment 735* were unable to get themselves ready for action.

On the same day the *1. Kompanie* repelled the attacks launched by the Allied infantry at the small forest, and the *2. Kompanie* shelled and destroyed an identified infantry assembly area west of the cemetery. To renew the assault, the *1. Kompanie* was attached to battle group *„Schönfeld"*, and the *2. Kompanie* was put under command of battle group *'Hildebrandt'* in the evening.

On the night from 8 to 9 February, at 0000 hours the battle groups *'Hildebrandt'* and *'Schönfeld'* started an attack again towards Aprilia.

At the beginning of the attack the assault guns of the *2. Kompanie*, acting as artillery, shelled resistance nests from 0015 hours. The assault of the *I. Bataillon* of *Grenadier-Regiment 725* ground to a halt again in the midst of Allied fire 500m south of their jump-off position.

117 *Kriegstagebuch der Panzer-Abteilung 103* (copy in author's possession), pp. 77-79.

According to the report submitted by the pioneers, they had been able to clear the road of mines up to Point 78 (500m north of Aprilia) only by 0400 hours.

At 0400 hours, *Leutnant* Spengler and the *2. Kompanie* rolled out of their positions and reached the perimeter of the infantry 500m north of the water tower of Aprilia. With his assault gun platoon, *Leutnant* Gründel carried the grenadiers lying on the ground with them and took the water tower at around 0600 hours. An Allied AFV was also knocked out there and several prisoners were taken and handed over to the grenadiers.

Most of the *2. Kompanie*, which had caught up with the others by then, mopped up the area of the water tower east of the settlement. The armoured unit requested pioneer support immediately but it had still not arrived. By contrast, according to the unit's history of the *3. Panzergrenadier-Division*, a pioneer platoon riding on top of the AFVs also joined the attack and 300 mines were cleared by them.[118]

Although originally left out from command duties during the combat fought by the two battle groups, the commander of *Panzer-Abteilung 103* decided to bring forward his *3. Kompanie* to strongpoint 'Spider' and assume command of the whole *Abteilung*. During the drive, the *Major* had to order the grenadiers of *Grenadier-Regiment 725* and a field reserve battalion out of the houses and send them forward. Assault gun platoon *'Gründel'* of the *2. Kompanie* would have resumed its attack towards Aprilia from an easterly direction but it ran into a minefield and was forced to stop its advance for the time being. The company had to take the northern entrance of Aprilia under fire from there.

Leutnant Spengler identified another potential route of approach towards Aprilia and then, by his own decision, broke into the settlement with assault gun platoon *'Gründel'* while accompanied by a few grenadiers.[119] At around 0730 hours he reached the southern perimeter of the town.[120] Most of the *2. Kompanie* and the *3. Kompanie*, which had also been put into action by *Major* Haen, caught up at around 1015 hours.

The StuG. III assault guns immediately took up securing positions along the roads running out of the settlement. By so doing, they were able to repel an Allied counterthrust supported by armour, during which the German assault guns knocked out four AFVs and a heavy AT gun.

Following that, the assault guns, in cooperation with a small number of German infantry, cleared Aprilia and took 40 prisoners. When they penetrated the settlement, the Germans exploited the situation that emerged after the failure of the Allied counterattack, while the Allied AFVs were retreating southwards.[121]

At 1045 hours *Major* Haen reported to the division that Aprilia was firmly held by the German troops. The *Major* put the slowly arriving grenadiers under his command and employing them, he transformed Aprilia into a defensive strongpoint.

---

118 *See* Dieckhoff, Gerhard: *3. Infanterie-Division – 3. Infanterie-Division (mot.) – 3. Panzergrenadier-Division* Cuxhaven, s.a., p. 294.

119 Those German soldiers probably belonged to the *III. Bataillon* of *Grenadier-Regiment 725*.

120 Dieckhoff, Gerhard: *3. Infanterie-Division – 3. Infanterie-Division (mot.) – 3. Panzergrenadier-Division* Cuxhaven, s.a., p. 294.

121 During a later discussion with the infantry, it emerged that a German grenadier reconnaissance patrol might have reached Aprilia in the early hours, but had been unable to gain a foothold in the settlement at that time.

The Allied infantry east of the settlement tried to get back in a southerly direction until 1200 hours but it proved to be extremely difficult for them in the midst of the HE shells and machine-gun fire of the assault guns.

In the afternoon, the StuG. III assault guns of *Panzer-Abteilung 103* repulsed infantry attacks from south and, at around 1500 hours, dispersed an armoured assembly area south of Aprilia and on the Cle Biadaretto road in a north-westerly direction.

The *II. Bataillon* of *Grenadier-Regiment 725* was brought to a halt in front of an Allied strongpoint established at Point 81 west of Aprilia and was unable – despite repeated orders to the contrary – to close the gap in the German front line before nightfall.

At 1530 hours the Allied AFVs attempted an attack from a southerly direction but the German artillery prevented them from deploying and they withdrew after nightfall.

On the same day, from 0100 hours the *1. Sturmgeschütz-Kompanie* (subordinated to battle group *'Schönfeld'*) provided fire support from the towel-shaped small forest for the infantry as they pushed forward. Nevertheless, the advance ground to a halt at Point 72 in ferocious fire. *Hauptmann der Reserve* Hinzpeter launched an attack at 0500 hours with six assault guns and 12 grenadiers of *Panzergrenadier-Regiment 104* riding on top of them, with the aim of eliminating the Allied strongpoint. The AFVs approached the Allied position to within 100m. At that point the grenadiers dismounted and assaulted a group of houses with the fire support of the assault guns. However, the Allies put up a resolute defence and the dozen Germans were unable to take the houses. As a result, the assault guns retreated to their previous position with the grenadiers reduced to six men. At 0600 hours the *Sturmgeschütz-Kompanie*, together with the I. *Bataillon* of *Grenadier-Regiment 735*, launched yet another attack on Point 72 and eliminated the resistance there during a short but fierce exchange of fire. Following that, the *1. Kompanie* fought its way to its designated positions immediately east of Ponte Guardapassi.

While pushing forward, the assault guns knocked out two heavy AT guns and took about 70 prisoners at a cost of one StuG. III knocked out. At 0745 hours the *Sturmgeschütz-Kompanie* observed an Allied armoured fighting vehicle behind a manor near Ponte Guardapassi and destroyed it with three shots.

The British and American troops made several attempts to retake Aprilia in the afternoon with about 70 AFVs – without infantry support – from south and southeast. The attack was repulsed by the concentrated fire of the German artillery, the assault guns of *Panzer-Abteilung 103* as well as the Hornisse tank destroyers of *schwere Panzerjäger-Abteilung 525*.

In the course of these attempts, a group of Allied armour (28 AFVs) launched an attack at around 1500 hours from the direction of Cle Biadaretto on the positions held by the *1. Kompanie* but withdrew in a south-easterly direction after two of their tanks had been knocked out. The *Sturmgeschütz-Kompanie* successfully shelled the Allied strongpoints identified south of the new main combat line before nightfall and then secured Aprilia from southerly and easterly directions.

On the same day the Allies lost 400 prisoners, 17 AFVs and four AT guns in the area of Aprilia.[122]

122 Dieckhoff, Gerhard: *3. Infanterie-Division – 3. Infanterie-Division (mot.) – 3. Panzergrenadier-Division* Cuxhaven, s.a., p. 296.

During the attack on Aprilia *Panzer-Abteilung 103* destroyed a total of eight Allied AFVs and four AT guns and took 110 prisoners. The unit lost *Leutnant* Cramme during the battle, who was killed in his assault gun when it received a hit by an AT gun, as well as *Leutnant* Sippel, who was seriously wounded by shell fragments and died in hospital on 20 February. Besides them, an additional nine German soldiers belonging to the armoured units were wounded. One StuG. III was written off as a total loss and another four assault guns were damaged in combat.[123]

On 10 February, the assault guns still secured the front line achieved from southerly and easterly directions under extremely heavy Allied artillery fire. During the evening hours Allied bombers and fighter-bombers raided Aprilia and its vicinity in several waves. The unit suffered no loss of vehicles. After nightfall more intensive fire activity began and this lasted throughout the night.

On 11 February at dawn it came to the German's attention from intercepted Allied radio traffic that, at 0500 hours, a counterthrust was to be anticipated in the direction of Aprilia.

At 0700 hours the Allies opened a barrage as artillery preparation before the attack on Aprilia jumped off. Taking advantage of the fog and the effect of the phosphorus smoke grenades that prevented the Germans from observing them and conducting fire, the American troops,[124] with the support of about 15 AFVs,[125] approached the settlement to within 1000m from a southerly direction. The combat vehicles had previously joined the artillery preparation and had shelled the southern perimeter of Aprilia at a distance of about 2km. The nerves of the German infantry – still inexperienced in fighting – frayed out in the midst of the violent fire and they gave up their positions to withdraw towards Aprilia.

However, the assault guns of *Panzer-Abteilung 103* held their positions firmly. The Germans were able to prevent the attack from gaining ground. Moreover, the *3. Kompanie* knocked out an Allied combat vehicle 1km south-east of Aprilia.

The advance of the American tanks was slowed by British AFVs that had been knocked out days before. Two companies of the 191st Tank Battalion – which had penetrated the German defences, partly among the buildings – ran out of ammunition and were forced to retreat at around noon.[126]

Due to the failure of the attack the Allies were carried out assaults on the German positions throughout the morning but these were repelled by the defenders.

At 1400 hours, following an artillery preparation, another attack was launched, supported by AFVs. Again, it was repulsed by the StuG. III assault guns after they had knocked out two combat vehicles and disabled two others.

---

123 For the dispatch written by *Major* Haen about the retaking of Aprilia on 9 February 1944 *see* the war diary of *Panzer-Abteilung 103!* In: *Kriegstagebuch der Panzer-Abteilung 103* (copy in author's possession), pp. 82-85.

124 Those were probably the 1st Battalion of the 179th Infantry Regiment of the US 45th Infantry Division and the M4 (Sherman) tanks of 191st Tank Battalion providing support for them. *See* Zaloga, Steven J.: Anzio 1944. Campaign 155, Osprey Publishing. Oxford, 2005. p. 52.

125 The American infantry was accompanied by the 'A' and 'B' companies of the 191st Tank Battalion. *See* Yeide, Harry: *The Infantry's Armor. The U.S. Army's Separate Tank Battalions in World War II.* Stackpole Books, Mechanicsburg, 2010. p. 79.

126 Zaloga, Steven J.: *Anzio 1944. Campaign 155, Osprey Publishing.* Oxford, 2005. p. 56., *and also* Yeide, Harry: *The Infantry's Armor. The U.S. Army's Separate Tank Battalions in World War II.* Stackpole Books, Mechanicsburg, 2010. p. 79. The rate of tank ammunition expenditure was surely increased by their participation in the artillery preparation which initiated the attack.

The Allies increased their artillery fire support and in another attack – which commenced at 1530 hours under the cover of fog – they approached to within 500m of the southern entrance to Aprilia. The German infantry evacuated its positions again, and according to the direct observation of *Leutnant* Spiegel from the *3. Kompanie*, they either surrendered or retreated towards Aprilia.

Nevertheless, the assault guns of the *2.* and the *3. Kompanien* took up the fight without the support of the grenadiers. A furious armoured battle ensued that lasted for twenty minutes, during which eight Allied AFVs were destroyed and the assaulting infantry was dispersed by HE shells and machine-gun fire. The *3. Kompanie* played a decisive role in this successful defensive battle as the focal point of the Allied attack was immediately in front of their positions.

The *1. Kompanie*, securing east of Aprilia, also joined the struggle despite being much farther away and, acting as artillery, shelled the combat formation of the Allied infantry. Despite firing at long range, the company knocked out an Allied tank turning towards south-east.

The German troops had effectively repelled the American attack by 1615 hours. The German assault guns jumped off to mount a counterthrust that inflicted heavy casualties on the retreating Allied infantry. Due to the serious losses suffered[127] the Allies didn't commence further attacks on that day.

The summary of the battle fought for the Anzio bridgehead made by the Anglo–American Allies, based on contemporary German documents, quotes the following German account about the day's fighting:

'As an enemy attack on Aprilia was expected the anti-tank defence in this sector was especially reinforced. Our infantry was in position on the southern edge of the village. Only 12 assault guns and several heavy anti-tank guns remained in Aprilia.

Although Aprilia was heavily shelled, our losses were comparatively small because the assault guns took cover behind the houses and waited for enemy tanks to come within close range before firing on them. The assault guns were very successful; 11 enemy tanks were destroyed, and 1 put out of commission. The fact that, despite repeated enemy attacks, the main line of resistance remained firm gives credit to the excellent registration of our artillery. The "Hornets"[128] due of their thin armour plating remained in the rear but were also very successful in the anti-tank defence. They destroyed enemy tanks at a distance of 2.5km.'[129]

In the day's fighting the Allies lost 38 POWs and 16 AFVs[130] in the area of Aprilia. Of these, *Panzer-Abteilung 103* destroyed 12 AFVs[131] and one AT gun, and heavily damaged an

127 The 1st battalion of the US 179th Infantry Regiment lost two-thirds of its combat strength that day. *See* Zaloga, Steven J.: *Anzio 1944. Campaign 155,* Osprey Publishing. Oxford, 2005. p. 52.

128 Those were German Hornisse heavy tank destroyers equipped with 8.8cm AT gun.

129 The German Operation at Anzio. Produced at GMDS by a combined British, Canadian and U.S. Staff, 1946. p. 44.

130 Dieckhoff, Gerhard: *3. Infanterie-Division – 3. Infanterie-Division (mot.) – 3. Panzergrenadier-Division* Cuxhaven, s.a., p. 296.

131 In the dispatch of *Panzer-Abteilung 103* dated 12 February 1944, there were only 11 knocked out AFVs due to an error in addition occurred while totalling figures. *See Kriegstagebuch der Panzer-Abteilung 103* (copy in author's possession), p. 89. On that day the two companies of the US 191st Tank Battalion lost five Sherman tanks respectively. *See* Yeide, Harry: *The Infantry's Armor. The U.S. Army's Separate Tank Battalions in World War II.* Stackpole Books, Mechanicsburg, 2010. p. 79.

additional two AFVs. *Leutnant* Gründel, who had been the first to penetrate Aprilia at the head of his assault gun platoon two days before, was killed by an artillery hit.

The night from 11 to 12 February began peacefully for the *2. and 3. Kompanien* as they performed security duties in Aprilia, and also for the *1. Kompanie* in position at Point 71, in the area of Ponte Guardapassi, apart from the occasional intensification of harassing fire by the Allied artillery and sporadic air-raids carried out by bombers and fighter-bombers.

At 0100 hours, however, German infantry positions were taken under violent machine-gun fire by the Allies. From this, the Germans were driven to the conclusion that yet another Allied attack was to be expected. Accordingly, *Leutnant* Spengler regrouped the assault guns of the *2. and 3. Kompanien* on the perimeter of Aprilia. At 0200 hours he also sent the two StuG. III assault guns that had arrived the previous evening, and had been held in reserve, to there.

One of the assault guns was put under command of *Leutnant* Spiegel at the south-western exit of the settlement, the other one took up a firing position on the right flank. As soon as the assault guns had taken up their designated positions, a handful of Allied tanks opened fire at a greater distance. However, the German assault guns remained silent, so that they wouldn't reveal the location of their favourably situated defensive positions. The machine guns of the German infantry were able to repel a later, and as it turned out, more forceful attack without intervention of the assault guns. At around 0500 hours the sounds of battle diminished.

During the day everything was peaceful in the area. In the morning, four Allied tanks tried to move from the south in a northerly direction, along the road bypassing Aprilia from west. With nothing to lose by trying, the assault guns opened fire at them at the very long range of 1800m, but failed to score a single hit. During the noon hours the commander of the *3. Panzergrenadier-Division*, accompanied by *Major* Haen, visited the defensive positions of *Panzer-Abteilung 103* and expressed his appreciation and gratitude to the personnel for their merit shown during the fighting of the previous days.

In the evening *Hauptmann der Reserve* Hinzpeter and *Leutnant* Zaunmüller were relieved by *Leutnant* Walz and *Leutnant* Spiegel.

On the night from 12 to 13 February no special event occurred. At 1400 hours the Allied artillery began to shell the southern perimeter of Aprilia again. Half an hour later fighter-bomber aircraft carried out an attack on the positions of *Panzer-Abteilung 103* but inflicted no losses.

At around 1500 hours the Allies fired smoke shells on the southern perimeter of Aprilia but, in the end, no attack was launched. From 1600 hours, periodic artillery harassing fire hammered the German positions.

However, in the early evening hours the positions held by the *1. Kompanie* were taken under fire by the Allied artillery in cooperation with naval guns. The intensity of the fire varied but, after 2100 hours, it intensified into a steady barrage.

In the evening *Major* Haen withdrew the *2. and 3. Kompanien* from Aprilia, relieving them with the four regrouped assault guns of the *1. Kompanie.* The latter assault guns moved out from Ponte Guardapassi during very heavy artillery fire. In spite of that, the regrouping was successfully carried out without any complication while concealed from the view of the Allies.

On 14 February, combat activity was limited to harassing fire, sporadic air attacks and a few failed assaults conducted by the Allies.

On the night from 14 to 15 February *Leutnant* Walz reported at one of the battalions of the *Infanterie-Lehr-Regiment* in Carroceto with two assault guns and was subordinated to the battalion. With the support of the StuG. III assault guns, the front line was pushed forward several hundred metres by the infantry in the area of Point 82, south of Carroceto.

During the morning, one of the assault guns of *Leutnant* Walz struck a mine in the area of the *Stazione* (railway station) and was immobilized due to the damage to the running gear.

In the afternoon, several soldiers of *Panzer-Abteilung 103* were awarded different kinds of decorations for their achievements shown during the fighting of the previous days. At the same time, *Major* Haen ordered all the officers and assault gun commanders – except for those of the four assault guns put into action – to assemble at the command post where he would brief them about a new, large-scale attack – codenamed '*Fischfang*'– on the Allied bridgehead and define tasks with greater precision.

In his speech the commander of the unit expressed his thanks for the unconditional devotion and the achievement shown during the battle for Aprilia. In addition, he gave utterance to his expectation that in this new operational phase opening right now, which would decisively influence the outcome of the war, each and every member of the unit would do his best and thoroughly fulfil his duty. He made it clear that he didn't expect his men to do the impossible but, as he put it, 'We must strive for the impossible to achieve the possible.'

According to the evaluation that can be found in the war diary of the unit, it was the achievements of *Panzer-Abteilung 103* that created the conditions that made the new offensive against the Allied bridgehead possible. That is to say, by retaking Aprilia and Carroceto and defending them, the AFVs secured the area for days during vicious combat. Furthermore, the assault guns provided their division with invaluable reconnaissance information concerning Allied troop movements.[132]

At 1800 hours *Panzer-Abteilung 103* reported to the division that they were ready for action. Two hours later, orders concerning the attack next day were issued.

In the afternoon and during the evening hours, the Allies continued to harass the German troops in the area of Aprilia and Carroceto by means of air raids and artillery harassing fire.

At around 2300 hours, a reconnaissance attempt made by the German infantry in the area of Carroceto prompted the Allies to respond with extremely violent artillery and small arms fire, which continued throughout the entire night with only occasional, short intermissions. Despite that, the Germans were able to tow away the assault gun of *Leutnant* Walz, that had struck a mine. *Feldwebel* Starost, the commander of the prime mover detachment of *Panzer-Abteilung 103*, bore the brunt of that recovery task.

On the same day the *1. Kompanie* of the armoured unit possessed 15 and the *2. Kompanie* 11 StuG. III assault guns respectively. The *3. Kompanie* had 10 assault guns and the staff of the battalion had three command tanks.[133]

132 See *Kriegstagebuch der Panzer-Abteilung 103* (copy in author's possession), p. 94.

133 NARA T312, R483 (*Armeeoberkommando 14*), F8074113.

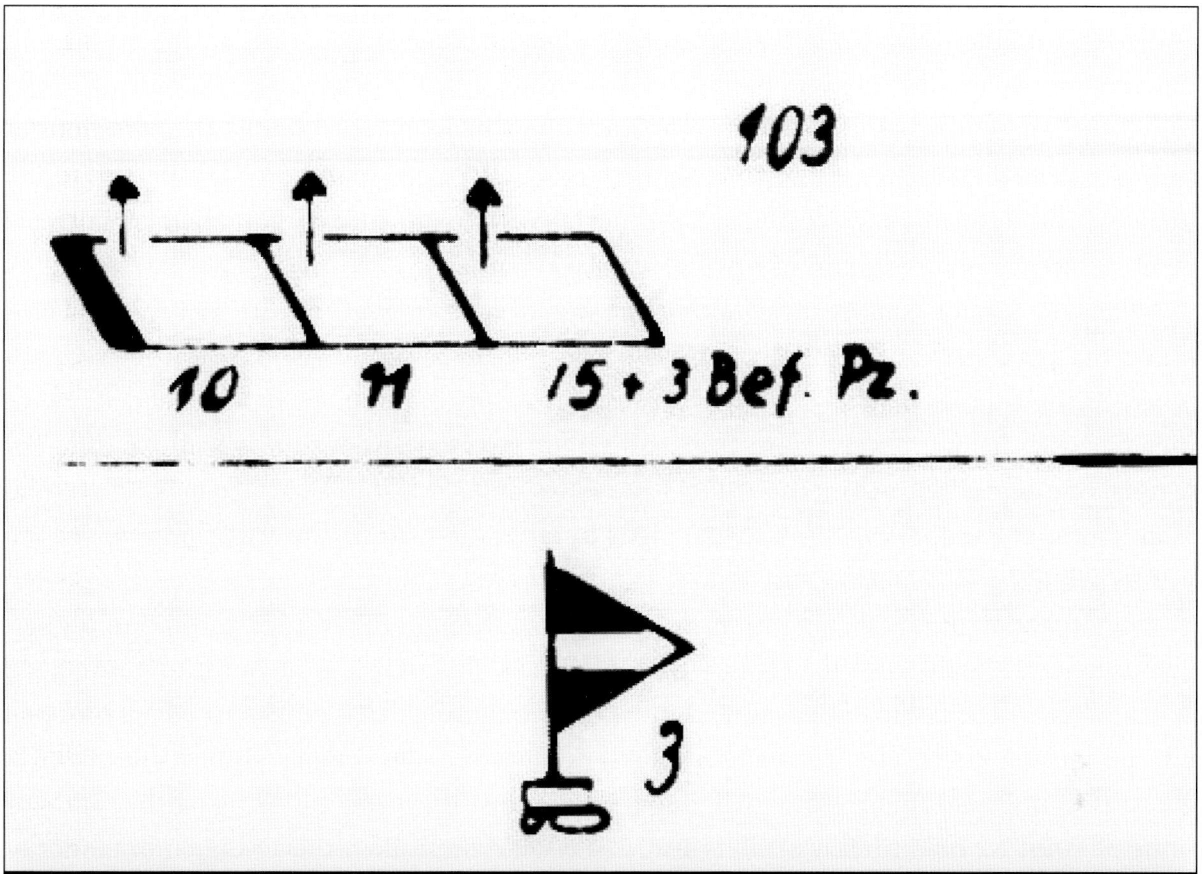

Order of battle of Panzer-Abteilung 103 on 15 February 1944

On 16 February at 0040 hours, *Panzer-Abteilung 103* moved out from the south-western foreground of Albano to take up its readiness positions. The unit had great difficulty moving forward because the only possible route of march was crammed with columns of vehicles belonging to two German divisions. On top of all that, the Allies contributed greatly to the chaos with their sporadic air attacks and artillery harassing fire. For all that, the German armoured unit reported at 0500 hours, that they had taken up their readiness position in the area of Carroceto.

At 0630 hours – following an intense artillery preparation – the German attack code-named '*Fischfang*' commenced.

In the sector of the *3. Panzergrenadier-Division, Infanterie-Lehr-Regiment* launched its attack from the southern foreground of Carroceto. After 30 minutes the direction of the German attack had been determined by the Allies who responded with violent artillery and mortar fire. The Allies had expected the German attack and had very skilfully organized their defence; they were well prepared.

As soon as *Infanterie-Lehr-Regiment* had jumped off, the *2. Kompanie* of *Panzer-Abteilung (Funklenk) 301* tried to make a breach in the Allied plan of fire with nine B IV radio-controlled demolition armoured vehicles but, due to the difficulties presented by the terrain and improperly employed tactics, the attempt failed.

The German infantry reached the southern slope of Point 82 with the fire support of the *3. Kompanie* of *Panzer-Abteilung 103*. Due to the almost impassable terrain, the assault guns were confined to the roads. As a result, the brunt of the fighting fell on the infantry.[134] Crossing the landmark, the lead battalion of *Infanterie-Lehr-Regiment* yet again came under heavy artillery fire and was unable to press forward owing to the flanking fire it received from well-established Allied positions[135] on their right as well as on their left. The neighbouring forces of the *715. Infanterie-Division* on their left hand side, having launched their attack from the southern foreground of Aprilia, were also halted.

When the assault guns of the *3. Kompanie* were drawn forward on the highway to Point 82 on the perimeter of the infantry, the Allies were fully aware of the danger the Germans posed to their defences: they threatened to achieve a penetration. In reply, Allied AT guns together with field and naval guns began to target the German positions in three different sectors, one behind the other. The artillery fire soon intensified into a barrage in which several assault guns of the *3. Kompanie* were damaged in rapid succession. The only thing to be done was to bring the *2. Kompanie* forward.

Leutnant Spengler's *2. Kompanie* made a bold dash through the combat formation of their own infantry, regardless of the artillery fire. However, the assault guns ran into a minefield at Point K23. The company engaged the Allied strongpoints, AT guns and AFVs on open terrain without cover. The German armoured combat vehicles fought without the slightest glimmer of hope of support from their grenadiers because they were still lying on the southern slope of Point 82 under heavy artillery fire. *Leutnant* Zaunmüller, the acting commander of the *3. Kompanie* was killed and another three assault gun commanders were wounded in the ferocious hail of artillery shells.

At around 1300 hours the Allied AFVs tried to halt the German assault guns by means of an outflanking manoeuver on the German's eastern flank. The StuG. IIIs fired on them at about 1800m: two Allied tanks were destroyed, another two were immobilized and their crews left them behind. The remaining Allied AFVs retreated southwards. The *1. Kompanie* remained in the area of Carroceto until 1300 hours, where two of its assault guns were disabled as a result of the ceaseless fighter-bomber attacks.

Allied combat vehicles commenced an attack in front of the positions held by the *2. Kompanie* at 1445 hours, on road Via Anziante. One of them was knocked out by the lead assault guns of the company.[136]

In the ceaseless Allied artillery and AT fire, the Germans were left with little option but to stop pushing forward and to secure the front line achieved from south, south-west and east. To that purpose, the assault guns of the *2.* and *3. Kompanie* were withdrawn to securing positions for the night.

On the night from 16 to 17 February, in accordance with the orders issued by the *LXXVI. Panzerkorps*, three armoured groups were formed in the sector of the corps, each composed

134 Dieckhoff, Gerhard: *3. Infanterie-Division – 3. Infanterie-Division (mot.) – 3. Panzergrenadier-Division* Cuxhaven, s.a., p. 299.

135 The sector was defended by the 157th and 179th Infantry Regiments of the US 45th Infantry Division, supported by 144 artillery guns, as well as the M10 tank destroyers of the 645th Tank-Destroyer Battalion, plus an M4 tank company of the 191st Tank Battalion. *See* Zaloga, Steven J.: *Anzio 1944. Campaign 155*, Osprey Publishing. Oxford, 2005. p. 63.

136 According to American sources the 191st Tank Battalion reported 15 German AFVs as knocked out on that day until 1800 hours, as well as seven lost Sherman tanks of their own. *See* Yeide, Harry: *The Infantry's Armor. The U.S. Army's Separate Tank Battalions in World War II.* Stackpole Books, Mechanicsburg, 2010. p. 79.

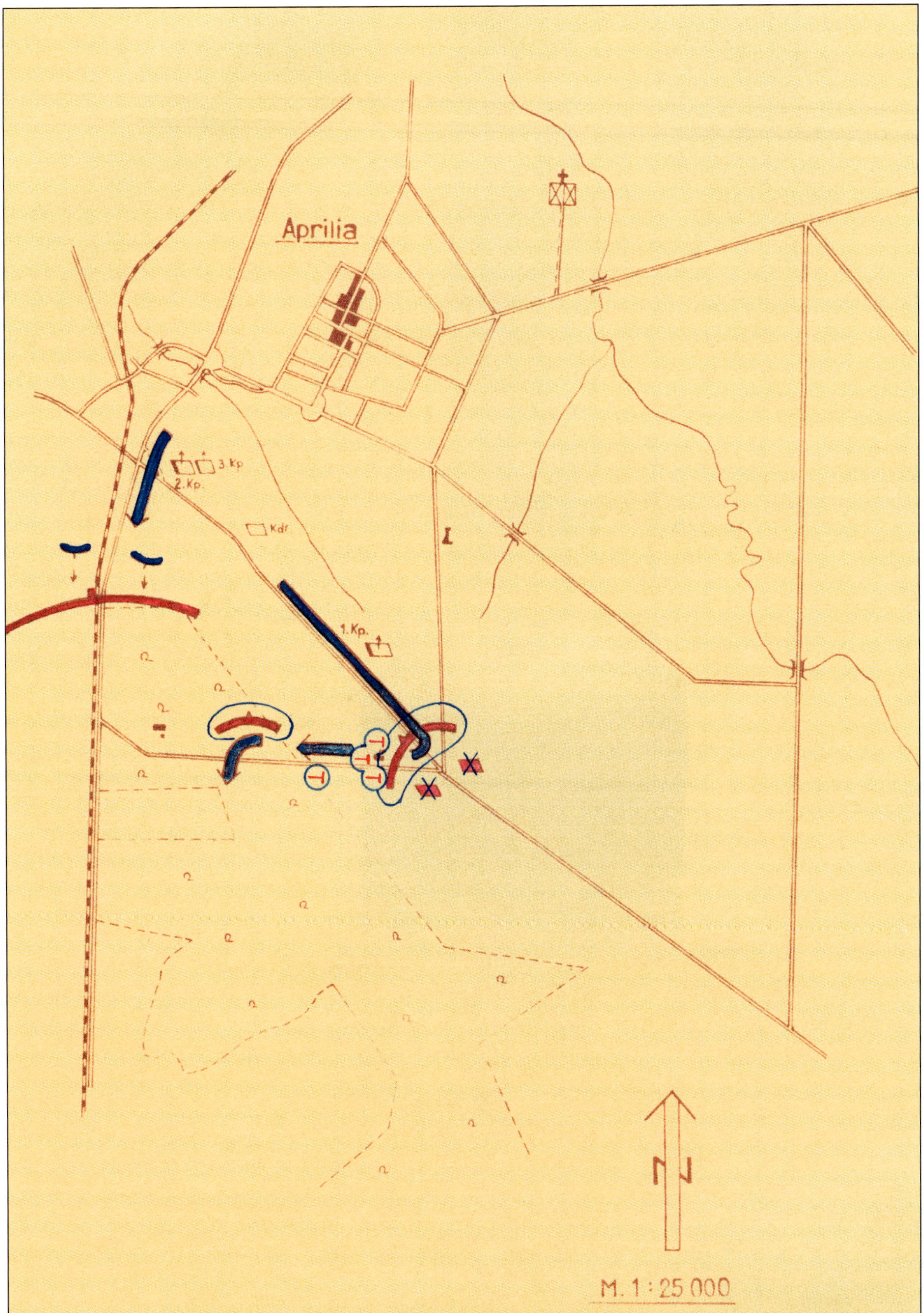

Situation map, 17 February 1944

of two Tiger heavy tanks, two Sturmpanzer IV assault tanks and two assault guns, plus B IV demolition armoured vehicles (radio-controlled by two assault guns). One of those mixed armoured groups was put under the command of *Major* Haen.

By express orders of the corps, those armoured groups were to break through the Allied front line in a southerly direction with the timing being set by the attacking German *3. Panzergrenadier* and *715. Infanterie* divisions respectively. However, the execution of this manoeuver failed due to the well-known '*tactical impossibility*' of putting armour into action at night. Moreover, in the course of the attempt, the Allied AT guns and AFVs knocked out both Tigers plus an assault tank and an assault gun in a very short while.

At sunrise *Major* Haen, on his own initiative, ordered the *1. Kompanie* of *Panzer-Abteilung 103* to attack from the area of Carroceto in a south-easterly direction in the sector of the *715. Infanterie-Division* to eliminate the danger of the flank attack once and for all. The *Sturmgeschütz-Kompanie* attacked an Allied tank group at the triple road junction and by knocking out three AFVs, destroyed it during a short firefight. Following that, the *1. Kompanie* received orders to turn westwards without delay and thereby roll up the Allied front line, which had been stabilized along the German line of communication, from the flank.

Elements of the *2. Kompanie* provided fire support for the assault guns of the *1. Kompanie* on the drive, taking up firing positions on the southern slope of Point 82. The manoeuvre precisely executed by the *1. Kompanie* caught the Allies by surprise and they lost 100 prisoners and four AT guns captured by the Germans.

Exploiting the success achieved by the *1. Kompanie*, *Leutnant* Spengler advanced southwards to Points K23 and K24 with the assault guns of the *2. Kompanie* despite the increasing danger to his western flank. Together with the AFVs of the *2. Kompanie*, the infantry of *Infanterie-Lehr-Regiment* pushed forward on a wide front closer towards the focus of the German attack, Highway 82, as did *Grenadier-Regiment (mot.) 29* which had been put into action to the east of them. By nightfall the Germans had successfully occupied the area of Carrocetello Creek and the east-west road 1200m north of Highway 82 in a most violent battle in the face of permanent Allied artillery fire superiority. During the day the assault guns of *Panzer-Abteilung 103* were damaged one after the other in the persistent, heavy artillery fire. By nightfall, only six StuG. III assault guns remained combat-ready in the whole unit. These were subordinated to the company commander, *Hauptmann der Reserve* Hinzpeter, and ordered to the east-west road. Despite the heavy artillery fire the *Sturmgeschütz-Kompanie* held its positions against Allied AFVs attacking from south-west, south and east.

On 18 February before noon, the combat-ready assault guns of *Panzer-Abteilung 103* were still defending their hard-won achievement and provided fire support for the assault squads of the *Infanterie-Lehr-Regiment* as they dashed towards Highway 82. Some of these squads did reach the line of the highway but were unable to gain a foothold because the Allied troops placed them under punishing flanking fire from both west and east.

In the afternoon, *Panzer-Abteilung 103* was reinforced by a platoon of Tiger heavy tanks and another platoon of Sturmpanzer IV assault tanks. These combat vehicles commenced an attack towards Highway 82 led personally by *Major* Haen. A kilometre to the north, the

Tiger heavy tanks engaged in a firefight with the Allied AFVs[137] in the course of which the combat vehicle of the platoon commander was disabled, cutting off all communications with the heavy tank platoon. Moreover, the AFV of the assault tank platoon was also damaged and as a result the commander was unable to submit further reports at a decisive moment in the battle. Upon that, *Major* Haen himself started off towards the three Tigers that were still combat-ready but was unable to send them to their designated positions as they were engaging Allied tanks that were attacking in superior in numbers. The German AFVs destroyed a total of eight Sherman tanks plus two AT guns during the battle.

On the night from 18 to 19 February, the combat-ready Tiger heavy AFVs were subordinated to armoured group *'Hinzpeter.'* At sunrise, the Allies launched a relief attack with the support of AFVs along the north-south road. However, this was perceived by the alert crews of the Tigers, and they knocked out a total of four Allied combat vehicles.

In the morning, *Panzer-Abteilung 103* received an additional five Panther tanks from the *I. Abteilung* of *Panzer-Regiment 4* as reinforcements. However, they were unable to make much use of them because four of the Panthers had either been disabled during their march down the Via Anziate by artillery fire or had become stuck. Although the fifth Panther did arrive at armoured group *'Hinzpeter'*, after an hour or so it made itself independent and retreated without receiving any orders, offering the excuse that it had to carry the wounded to the rear.

In the afternoon hours the Allies attempted another armoured counterthrust during which, by making use of a smokescreen, they approached armoured group *'Hinzpeter'* to within 800m. However, the four attacking Sherman tanks were annihilated by the German combat vehicles in a short firefight.

By dawn on 20 February, the continuing heavy Allied artillery fire had damaged more of the German assault guns. By morning, only one StuG. III of *Panzer-Abteilung 103* had been left forward in a securing position. To substitute the damaged AFVs of the unit, the assault guns of *Panzer-Abteilung (Funklenk) 301* were ordered into the positions.

On the same day *Leutnant* Beschnidt took over command of the *2. Kompanie*. Six NCOs were sent to *Panzer-Ersatz-und Ausbildungs-Abteilung 10* located in Zinten.

To mislead enemy reconnaissance and compel the Allies to regroup their forces, *Panzer-Abteilung 103* received orders to stage mock troop movements for several days towards Ardea. The task was carried out by the soldiers of the unit under command of *Leutnant* Kannegiesser.

On 21 February, during the early hours, the crew members of the only combat-ready assault gun of *Panzer-Abteilung 103* captured an Allied AT gun together with its prime mover. The StuG. III remained in its securing position until 24 February, assigned to *Panzer-Abteilung (Funklenk) 301.*

On 23 February, in the evening, *Panzer-Abteilung 103* still possessed only one combat-ready StuG. III plus a command tank.[138]

---

137 Those were probably the M4 tanks of the 'H' company of the 1st Armored Regiment of the US 1st Armored Division. See Zaloga, Steven J.: Anzio 1944. Campaign 155, Osprey Publishing. Oxford, 2005. p. 55.

138 NARA T312, R483 (*Armeeoberkommando 14*), F8074645.

On the night from 24 to 25 February, that single assault gun was also pulled out from the front line.

During the fighting from 16 to 20 February, the personnel of *Panzer-Abteilung 103* fought with distinction once again. According to an evaluation made by the commander of the unit, it had proved a worthy successor to its predecessor of the same name that had been annihilated at Stalingrad. In the ceaseless Allied artillery fire, often joined by the heavy artillery of the cruisers anchoring in Anzio Bay, the German AFVs had to hold out against an enemy superior to them both numerically and in terms of materiel. Moreover, the Allies were waiting for the attack of the German assault guns with AFVs and AT guns established in well-chosen firing positions. The Allied counterthrusts were repelled one after another by the gun and machine-gun fire of the combat vehicles of *Panzer-Abteilung 103.* German infantry often received important, partly psychological, aid from the assault guns in the midst of the in-pouring Allied artillery fire.

The battalion surgeon of *Panzer-Abteilung 103, Oberarzt* Dr Meyer, fulfilled his commitments conscientiously and attended to those in need of medical help from other units as well as his own. For example on 18 February, all 82 wounded receiving medical assistance belonged to the *Infanterie-Lehr-Regiment.* The battalion surgeon was awarded the Iron Cross 2nd Class and then 1st Class in a very short period of time.

By that time, *Panzer-Abteilung 103* had destroyed 52 Allied AFVs and 12 AT guns and taken 200 prisoners during the battle fought at the Nettuno bridgehead. During that period of time, its own casualties were 17 KIA (including five officers), five MIA (including one officer), 33 wounded transported to hospitals (including two officers) as well as eight wounded who remained at the unit (including one officer) – a total of 63 men.[139]

Most of the assault guns disabled by Allied fire and the extremely unfavourable terrain could be put into action after having undergone extensive maintenance and time-consuming repairs. Sometimes working on more than 30 combat vehicles simultaneously, the unit's repair personnel laboured practically day and night. Between 29 January and 24 February the platoon repaired 29 heavily damaged StuG. IIIs. The maintenance detachments of the companies tried to relieve the workshop platoon by performing minor repairs. Nine StuG. III assault guns had to be written off as total losses during the fighting.

The commitment of the supply subunits was also exemplary: despite the artillery fire and the constant attacks of fighter-bombers they transported food, ammunition and fuel to the AFVs fighting on the front line.

On 26 February in the afternoon, a column of eight vehicles drove via Pavona and Zolforata towards Ardea. From that settlement *Leutnant* Kannegiesser moved some of the cars with their lights on in the western and south-western foreground of Ardea, while the others – with their lights on, too – were quartered in Ardea. During their march, these vehicles did not receive a single hit, either on the way to their destination or on their return journey.

On 27 February in the afternoon, this deceptive, mocking manoeuvre was repeated by 18 vehicles of the unit. However, it was raining ceaselessly and the terrain became impassable.

---

139 *Kriegstagebuch der Panzer-Abteilung 103* (copy in author's possession), p. 103.

Consequently they were forced to move exclusively on the road running from Ardea towards south-east. This time the column did receive Allied artillery harassing fire on several occasions but this inflicted no losses.

On 28 February vehicle movements continued on the roads that had dried out to the east of Ardea. Although these movements were observed by Allied air reconnaissance, and the roads were partly surveyed by the Allies, the columns were not placed under fire.

On 1 March *Major* Haen assumed command of the tank destroyer course provided by the *3. Panzergrenadier-Division*[140] during which the grenadiers and pioneers of the division also received training, lasting for four days, on fighting-down AFVs in close combat. All German AFVs in service were presented to them and they made themselves familiar with the everyday life of the German armoured troops. After that they practised close combat using man-portable AT grenade launchers *(Faustpatrone, Panzerfaust),* man-portable AT rocket launchers *(Ofenrohr)* and pioneer satchel charges. In this way the grenadiers and pioneers were rapidly familiarized with these anti-tank weapons.

On the same day, two newly assigned officers arrived at the unit: *Oberleutnant* Geisser[141] and *Leutnant* Göb. *Oberleutnant* Johl was assigned as the gas defence officer of the unit, and *Leutnant* Walther as the investigating officer. Simultaneously, *Oberleutnant* Häusser and *Leutnant* Grant, both recovering from serious wounds, were transferred to *Panzer-Ersatz-und Ausbildungs-Abteilung 10.*

In the evening *Panzer-Abteilung 103* already had 10 combat-ready assault guns and a command tank.[142]

On 2 March, *Major* Haen summoned company commanders for a meeting. He issued orders to provide ample quarters for the companies, especially for the crew members of the assault guns returning from the front line. Moreover, the commander of *Panzer-Abteilung 103* allowed the personnel to spend their leave in Rome, where they would have the opportunity for bathing and recreation.

The problem concerning the actual assault gun strength of the unit was also resolved. The nine StuG. IIIs that had been destroyed were cancelled from the list of equipment and the remaining 33 assault guns were distributed proportionately among the companies so that each company now had 11 of them. Of those, 12 assault guns plus a command tank were combat-ready that evening.[143]

Major Haen also ordered that in each company the assault gun of the company commander and the one held in his reserve, plus the StuG. III of the senior platoon commander with an additional one of his platoon (making a total of four AFVs per company), were to be equipped with FuG2 radio receiver/transmitter sets in addition to the FuG5 transceivers already installed in the vehicles.[144]

140 Besides, he was also in charge of organizing the whole AT defence plan of the division. *See* Dieckhoff, Gerhard: *3. Infanterie-Division – 3. Infanterie-Division (mot.) – 3. Panzergrenadier-Division* Cuxhaven, s.a., p. 302.

141 According to the war diary of the *3. Panzergrenadier-Division, Oberleutnant* Hans Geisser was transferred to the unit together with *Oberleutnant* Wilhelm Broich as of 15 November 1943. *See* NARA T315, R173 (*3. Panzergrenadier-Division*), F000936.

142 NARA T312, R483 (*Armeeoberkommando 14*), F8074593.

143 NARA T312, R483 (*Armeeoberkommando 14*), F8074586.

144 *Kriegstagebuch der Panzer-Abteilung 103* (copy in author's possession), p. 106.

Leutnant Walther was put in charge of taking care of the graves of the soldiers of *Panzer-Abteilung 103* killed in action and buried in the German Heroes' Cemetery in Rome.

On the night from 5 to 6 March, the *1. Kompanie* was returned to the front line from its quartering area with eight assault guns. Five of the StuG. IIIs were ordered to strongpoint 'Spider', 1-1,5 kilometres north of Aprilia as divisional reserve. The other three combat vehicles were held in corps reserve, under the command of *Leutnant* Walz, in the area of Campoleone and were given the task of intervening on a specific obstacle line should the Allied tanks break through.

The three assault guns also provided efficient fire support for the numerous assault attempts conducted by the *Infanterie-Lehr-Regiment.* By so doing, the AFVs also contributed to the fact that the Allies became unsure of German intentions. Moreover, those attempts successfully pushed the front line out a little, and improved the positions. In the evening *Panzer-Abteilung 103* had 12 combat-ready assault guns and two command tanks.[145]

On 8 March for example, the northern perimeter of the small forest of Grandi was successfully taken and strongpoints were established there.

During those days, besides their harassing fire, the Allied artillery contented itself with carrying out surprise fire attacks, particularly on German supply lines.

Incessant rain saturated the terrain, confining the assault guns to the roads.

In the evening *Panzer-Abteilung 103* had 13 combat-ready assault guns and two command tanks.[146]

On 9 March the number of combat-ready AFVs increased further. By the evening, 15 assault guns and two command tanks were combat-ready.[147]

On the night from 10 to 11 March, the assault guns of the *2. Kompanie* relieved the *1. Kompanie.* This task was successfully completed without illumination other than moonlight, and therefore remained unnoticed by the Allies. One of the five assault guns at strongpoint 'Spider' was drawn forward as an artillery communication vehicle, and was placed on the road running on the embankment at Reference Point 396.

During the morning, the positions held by the assault guns received heavy artillery fire which was extremely violent in the area of strongpoint 'Spider'.

In the evening *Major* Haen celebrated his 29th birthday with the officers of *Panzer-Abteilung 103.*

On 12 March an honour platoon of the unit attended the ceremony held in the German Heroes' Cemetery in Rome commemorating Heroes' Day. The division commander, *Generalleutnant* Gräser, and other commanders of the unit lit candles at the tomb of the division's unknown soldiers.

As far as the assault guns at the front line were concerned, nothing much changed on that or the following day. The Allied artillery fire intensified only during the evening of 13 March; on several occasions this was accompanied by concentrated British machine-gun fire. The Germans concluded that an attack should be anticipated but, at around midnight, the firing diminished and from then on the night passed peacefully.

145 NARA T312, R483 (*Armeeoberkommando 14*), F8074567.

146 NARA T312, R483 (*Armeeoberkommando 14*), F8074556.

147 NARA T312, R483 (*Armeeoberkommando 14*), F8074551.

On that day *Panzer-Abteilung 103* had four man-portable rocket launchers and 40 *Faustpatrone* at its disposal for training purposes.[148]

On 13 March *Hauptmann* Fischer was ordered to attend a battalion commanders' course and *Leutnant* Bothe a company commanders' course, both at the *Panzertruppenschule* in Putlos.

On the same day, and on the following day, *Oberleutnant* Geisser reconnoitred routes for the assault guns in the area of Montaldo, Valentano, Tuscania, Vetrella and Tarquinia, should the Allies effect another surprise landing.

On 14 March the assault guns of the *2. Kompanie* that had been put into action were repeatedly attacked as Allied fighter-bombers, exploiting the improving weather conditions, attacked in the area of Aprilia and also strafed the supply routes. Artillery activity was intensified on both sides during the night but otherwise nothing of any significance happened.

On that day, 10 assault guns were taken over by *Panzer-Abteilung 103* from *Panzer-Abteilung 129.* However, the combat vehicles were in such dire technical condition that they had to undergo thorough overhaul by the workshop platoon before they were ready to be used in combat. Following that, three of them were issued to each of the *1.* and *2. Kompanien* and four were allocated to the *3. Kompanie.* In the evening, *Panzer-Abteilung 103* had 20 combat-ready assault guns and two command tanks.[149]

Also on 14 March, the tank destroyer company of the division was established. *Panzer-Abteilung 103* was in charge of raising and equipping the new unit. Without any official TOE, one officer, 22 NCOs and 99 enlisted men were to be assigned as personnel. Its combat echelon was made up of two platoons of two squads each with two teams in each squad.

To improve its mobility, efforts were made to equip the tank destroyer company with smaller off-road vehicles so that the teams with their weapons could reach the front line as motorized detachments. To that purpose they employed the small British armoured ammunition carriers (Universal Carrier) captured, and repaired, on a previous front line by *Panzer-Abteilung 103.* These tracked vehicles, which also offered protection against shell fragments, had been used to carry supplies to the assault gun battalions for a short while and had already proven themselves among the shell-holes and on rough terrain.

Major Haen entrusted the task of furnishing the new company with those small armoured vehicles to *Inspekteur* Schlegel, the engineer of *Panzer-Abteilung 103.* Several armoured vehicles of that type lay scattered on the terrain in the area of Aprilia and of these, some of which seemed to be repairable. The German engineer selected the best of them and had his prime mover detachment remove them under Allied fire – 18 of these versatile vehicles were successfully recovered.

The workshop platoon set to work immediately to make the small armoured vehicles combat-ready. Initially, this seemed to be an impossible mission but 11 of these British vehicles were successfully made combat-ready without causing a delay in the repair of the assault guns that had dropped out of service. Vehicles that had been little more than piles of knocked-out, shapeless metal scattered on the battlefield now looked new. The repaired

148 NARA T312, R483 (*Armeeoberkommando 14*), F8074357.

149 NARA T312, R483 (*Armeeoberkommando 14*), F8074526.

British vehicles were fitted with brackets for carrying the AT weapons and ammunition and finished with a coat of camouflage paint. They also carried the German national insignia. Having been taken over by the tank destroyer company, several test runs were successfully completed before the vehicles were put into use. Besides them, the company also received a car and two motorcycles (also captured from the British) from *Panzer-Abteilung 103,* plus three trucks from the division.

Meanwhile, *Leutnant* Walther, the orderly officer of *Panzer-Abteilung 103,* saw to it that the essential weapons would be obtained. Despite encountering some difficulty, he successfully provided the unit with the following items: 40 bayonets, 40 Kar 98 carbines, 22 MP 38/40 submachine guns, 35 Polish and Belgian pistols, five MG 42 machine guns, 26 man-portable AT rocket launchers with a total of 305 rockets, 160 man-portable AT grenade launchers, 12 pairs of 6×30 binoculars, and all the ammunition, incendiary bottles, smoke hand grenades, smoke candles, AT mines and incendiary charges needed for them.

With the expert help of one of its NCOs, the armoured unit established the office of the tank destroyer company, as well as its accounting, weapons and equipment registry. Medical personnel were provided by the division.

Simultaneous with the work carried out to equip and organize the unit, the company started training with AT weapons.

On 15 March in the evening *Panzer-Abteilung 103* had only 15 assault guns and two command tanks combat-ready.[150]

By morning 16 March, the assault guns of the *3. Kompanie* relieved the *2. Kompanie* carrying out securing tasks behind the front line.

During the days that followed no infantry action occurred; the only perceptible sign of war was the heavy harassing fire of the Allied artillery. The German reconnaissance observed that the Allies were laying mines ahead of their front line, stretching barbed wire and fortifying their positions by various means.

In the evening *Panzer-Abteilung 103* had again 20 combat-ready StuG. III assault guns and two command tanks.[151]

On 17 March, the number of combat-ready assault guns had increased by the evening. At that time not less than 22 StuG. IIIs and two command tanks were combat-ready.[152]

On 19 March, at 0820 hours, the first (operational) staff officer of the *3. Panzergrenadier-Division* gave *Panzer-Abteilung 103* a call and informed them that on the right flank, at the connecting point between the *65. Infanterie-Division* and the *4. Fallschirmjäger-Division* the Allies had launched an attack. Readiness to march was ordered immediately at the armoured unit. At 0910 hours the *1.*and *2. Kompanie* (with a total of 20 assault guns) were ready to start off. The *3. Kompanie,* which was performing security duties, hadn't been pulled out of their forward positions. In the end the alert was called off at 1200 hours.

150 NARA T312, R483 (*Armeeoberkommando 14*), F8074519.
151 NARA T312, R483 (*Armeeoberkommando 14*), F8074515.
152 NARA T312, R483 (*Armeeoberkommando 14*), F8074509.

On 20 March, by the evening hours, a third command tank had also been declared combat-ready.[153]

On 21 March in the evening, *Panzer-Abteilung 103* had 25 assault guns and three command tanks operational.[154]

On the night from 21 to 22 March, one of the assault gun platoons of the *1. Kompanie*, under command of *Leutnant* Kannegiesser, was ordered into the sector of the *65. Infanterie-Division* in the area of Colle Nuove Tuffeli. The platoon was held in corps reserve and came under the command of *Panzerjäger-Abteilung 165.* The rest of the assault guns belonging to the *1. Kompanie* were sent to the area of strongpoint 'Spider' where they formed a force (of the *3. Panzerjäger-Division*) reserved for a counterthrust. One of the StuG. IIIs performed communications and artillery-observer duties behind the main combat line of the *I.* and *II. Bataillone* of the *Infanterie-Lehr-Regiment.*

During the days that followed, the sector was calm, apart from the usual artillery fire. Only the reconnaissance patrols and assault squads of both sides remained active. During those German attempts, it was impossible to put the assault guns into action because they were confined to paved roads due to the sodden, muddy terrain.

Meanwhile the assault guns that had been sent out liaised between the artillery and the infantry.

On 24 March, the German *14. Armee* had the following combat-ready armoured strength[155]:

Unit	Panzer III	Panzer IV	Panther	Tiger	Flamm-panzer	Assault gun
Sturmpz.-Abt. 216						35
26. Panzer-Div.	5	51			7	
29. Pz.Gren.-Div.	8	18				
3. Pz.Gren.-Div.						25
I./Pz.-Regiment 4			40			
s. Pz. Abt. 508				32		
Fallsch. StuG-Abt. XI						17 (Italian-made)
Total	13	69	40	32	7	77

153 NARA T312, R483 (*Armeeoberkommando 14*), F8074490.

154 NARA T312, R483 (*Armeeoberkommando 14*), F8074485.

155 The German Operation at Anzio. Produced at GMDS by a combined British, Canadian and U.S. Staff, 1946. p. 86.

On 26 March, the *1. Kompanie*, located at strongpoint 'Spider' and at the *I. Bataillon* of *Infanterie-Lehr-Regiment*, was relieved by the eight assault guns of the *2. Kompanie*. However, the assault gun platoon sent into the sector of the *65. Infanterie-Division* remained in its position according to orders it had received.

Clear weather and cloudless sky were favourable for Allied air activity, especially to the missions flown by reconnaissance aircraft. From the smoke screen laid down on the coastal area, the Germans concluded that additional troops had been disembarked by the Allies. In the evening, *Panzer-Abteilung 103* already had 26 assault guns and three command tanks operational.[156]

On 27 March in the evening, *Panzer-Abteilung 103* possessed 27 combat-ready StuG. IIIs and three command tanks.[157]

On 28 March at dawn, the Germans blew up the church tower and the water tower of Aprilia to deny Allied artillery observers two significant points of reference.

At night the three assault guns arriving at strongpoint 'Spider' moved into the area of Carroceto after nightfall and took up quarters there. In the evening, *Leutnant* Beschnidt reconnoitred the surrounding terrain and concluded that the terrain south-west of Aprilia was still impassable for the AFVs and that they were able to move only on the roads. Consequently no Allied armoured attack was anticipated despite the milder weather conditions.

On 29 March, *Oberfähnrich* Grafe was awarded the German Cross in Gold for the merit he showed during the battle fought along the River Volturno and at the Nettuno bridgehead. Simultaneously, news was received that second lieutenants Spengler and Zaunmüller, both killed in action, had been promoted to first lieutenants posthumously.

By orders of *Panzer-Abteilung 103* an additional assault gun platoon was sent from the *1. Kompanie* into the sector of the *65. Infanterie-Division* on that day. The platoon had been held in reserve at the *II. Bataillon* of the *Infanterie-Lehr-Regiment.* The other assault gun platoon that had been ordered there previously was still held in reserve for a counterthrust. Since there was no natural cover nearby, the Germans were forced to dig-in the StuG. IIIs.

On 30 March, and on the following day, the two assault gun platoons reconnoitred the area to find proper routes of march and firing positions should they be required to carry out counterthrusts towards Buon Riposo and Via Nettunes.

In the clear weather, Allied reconnaissance aircraft circled above the positions of the assault guns. The assault guns were able to avoid being located by the enemy only by thorough camouflage measures.

In the evening, *Panzer-Abteilung 103* had 28 assault guns and three command tanks operational.[158]

On the night from 30 to 31 March, the *3. Kompanie* relieved the assault guns of the *2. Kompanie* which was performing security duties ahead. On the way back, the crews of the German AFVs saw extensive fires in the coastal area.

---

156 NARA T312, R483 (*Armeeoberkommando 14*), F8074463.

157 NARA T312, R483 (*Armeeoberkommando 14*), F8074457.

158 NARA T312, R483 (*Armeeoberkommando 14*), F8074444.

On 1 April, the commander of the division, *Generalleutnant* Gräser, inspected the tank destroyer company commanded by *Leutnant* Raue. Besides the whole of the command staff of the division, visitors came from the corps, the army, and also from the army group, to inspect the newly established subunit. The company lined up on an open area with its vehicles, all of them captured from the enemy – as *Major* Haen deliberately emphasized in his oral report.

Following the report to the divisional commander, the company demonstrated the manoeuvrability of its vehicles, proving that it was not only well equipped but also excellently drilled and disciplined. The visitors also had the chance to take a good look at the teams' equipment and weaponry.

A short survey of the armoured tactics presently used both sides of the front line followed before a platoon of the tank destroyer company demonstrated its skills by staging a mock encounter with enemy combat vehicles. To make the demonstration more realistic, the prime mover detachment of *Panzer-Abteilung 103* provided four knocked-out Sherman tanks they had recovered from the battlefield during out an arduous night-time mission. The mobility of two Sherman tanks had been restored by the workshop platoon. During the exercise, the tank destroyer teams let the moving tanks come close to their anti-tank dugouts then disabled them with man-portable AT rocket launchers and an AT grenade launcher.

Afterwards, the visitors were informed about the weapons used by the tank destroyer teams and were presented with the opportunity of examining them at close quarters.

The anti-tank rocket launcher team in position on 1 April 1944

Nine armoured troop carriers of the tank destroyer company lined up on 1 April 1944

An armoured troop carrier of the tank destroyer company with the division's tactical symbol (left) and company's symbol (right)

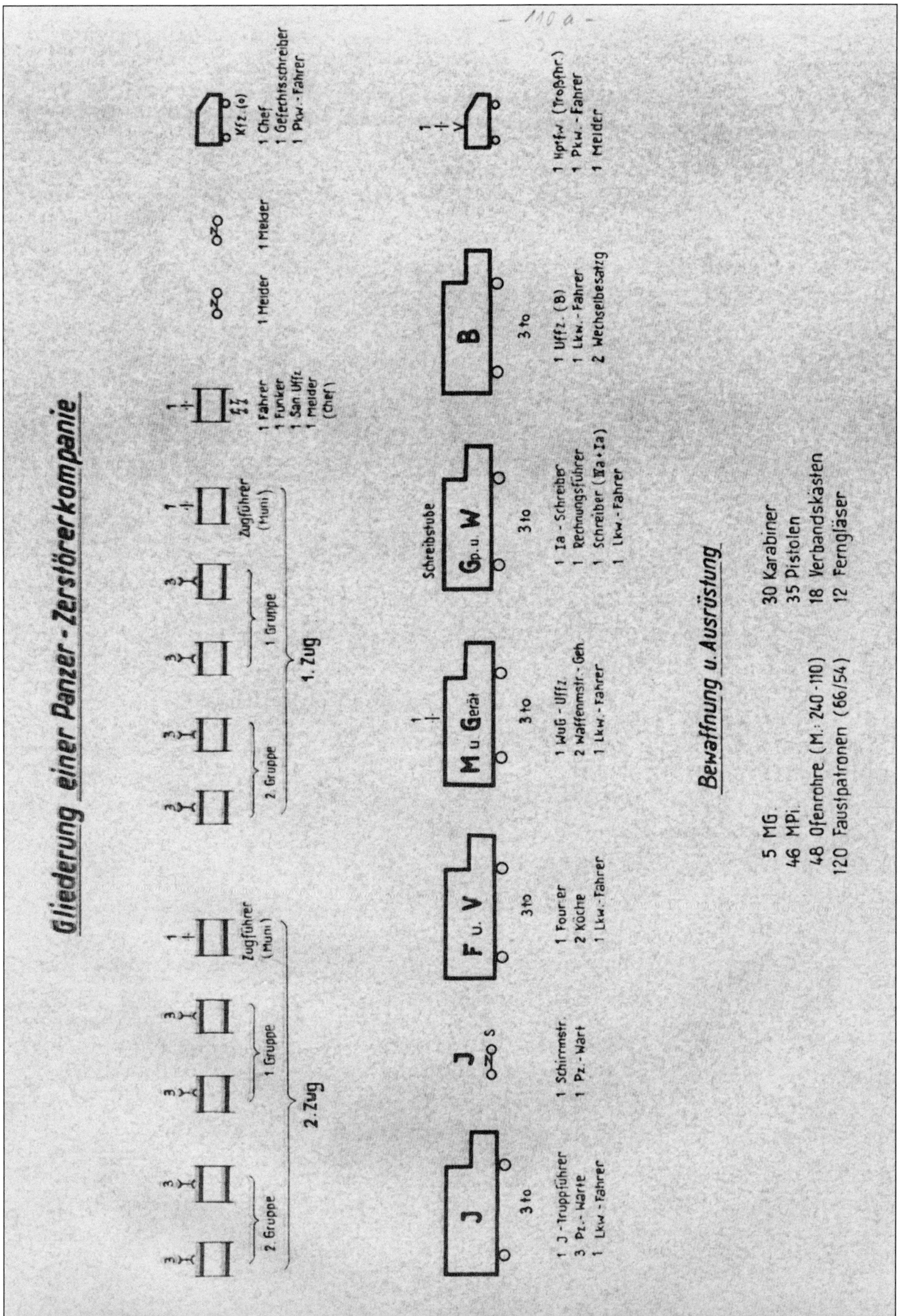

Order of battle of the tank destroyer company

The second demonstration depicted the offensive combat of two infantry assault squads reinforced by a tank destroyer section making an attack on an enemy rear guard that was supported by an AFV. During the mock battle it became evident that tank destroyer weapons were able to provide excellent support for the infantry during an attack not only by fighting down the AFV, but also by destroying built-out nests of resistance.

Generalleutnant Gräser expressed his thanks to the personnel for that entire training maneuver he had seen and for the hard work that had preceded the demonstration while still working within the framework of the divisional daily orders. *Major* Haen passed on *Generalleutnant* Gräser's thanks to the personnel concerned in his own daily order.

As the tank destroyer company demonstrated their skills in the mock battle, the two assault gun platoons of the *1. Kompanie* that were already in action linked up with the crews of other AT detachments fighting in their sector, especially with the personnel of *Panzerjäger-Abteilung 165.* Although the intensity of the Allied artillery fire had not diminished in any way, the platoons got on with building their bunkers. During his inspection, the commander of the *1. Kompanie* ordered the involvement of already established positions in the defensive plan.

On 5 April, the personnel of the two assault gun platoons reconnoitred the area again in preparation for the execution of probable counterthrusts.

On that day, orders were received from the division according to which 50 men were to be sent daily to the so-called Position 'C' to build machine-gun nests, bridges and infantry positions.

During the first days of April, only the Allied artillery fire blighted the life of the *3. Kompanie* in their securing positions. A few assault guns suffered repairable damage by indirect hits.

On 7 April, the assault guns of the *2. Kompanie* relieved those of the *3. Kompanie.* On the same day the adjutant of *Panzer-Abteilung 103, Leutnant* Schwäpenheuer, was promoted to the rank of *Oberleutnant* (first lieutenant).

On 8 April, the tank destroyer company achieved its first success: one of its teams in action on the main combat line knocked out a Sherman tank with armoured support and killed the crew as they attempted to abandon the tank.

In the noon hours, the Allied artillery poured destructive fire from large-calibre guns onto the command post of the *Infanterie-Lehr-Regiment.* Not only did the buildings collapse under the terrific fire, but the cannon of a StuG. III assault gun from *Panzer-Abteilung 103* was also damaged. However, German radio traffic was not disrupted during the artillery fire.

On 9 April, an AFV sent forward to make observations identified Allied artillery positions that were subsequently, and effectively, shelled by the German artillery.

On 10 April, *Leutnant* Müller was appointed commander of the reconnaissance platoon.

In the evening, personnel of *Panzer-Abteilung 103,* who had not been sent into action, attended a field service in the church of Cecchina.

The Germans observed that Allied vehicular traffic had intensified and that fortification efforts had been accelerated in their positions.

On the night from 11 to 12, the *Luftwaffe* carried out air attacks on Anzio and Nettuno, after which the Germans observed extensive fire and smoke.

Despite warmer, and windy, weather the terrain was still unsuitable for employing AFVs.

On 13 April, strongpoint 'Spider' and the surrounding area was hammered by violent Allied surprise fire-attacks without loss to the Germans.

Leutnant Müller was appointed sports officer of the unit on that day.

On 14 April, in the early hours, the *3. Kompanie* (with 12 assault guns) again relieved the *2. Kompanie.* Radio communication were established between the assault guns at strongpoint 'Spider', the assault gun platoon at the railway station of Aprilia, the advanced observer AFV at the *II. Bataillon* of *Infanterie-Lehr-Regiment,* the staff of *Panzer-Abteilung 103* (and its own communications AFV located at the divisional command post), and both platoons of the *1. Kompanie.* Moreover, a captured British Universal Carrier, equipped with a FuG 5 radio, was stationed at each of the relevant grenadier regiment command posts. Therefore *Major* Haen had a whole communications network at his disposal in the sector of his own division and also radio connection to his two assault gun platoons employed in the sector of the neighbouring *65. Infanterie-Division.*

On 15 April, the commander of *Panzer-Abteilung 103* summoned his officers for a meeting. He informed them of the situation and pointed out that the unit would surely be at the focal point of a forthcoming Allied attack and that, with this in mind, they should achieve the highest possible level of combat efficiency. In this context, it was imperative for all officers to provide continuous training for their men, to inform them about the political situation and to devote special attention to counterintelligence but with regard to the feelings of the Italian population. Severe measures were to be taken against panic-mongers.

On that day the last tank destroyer course was completed. A total of 750 soldiers had been trained in close-combat against armour during nine four-day courses conducted by *Panzer-Abteilung 103.*

On 16 April, by orders received, an assault gun platoon of the *1. Kompanie* reconnoitred the terrain to locate a suitable site for a strongpoint to be established in the area of Buon Riposo.

The assault guns of the *3. Kompanie,* performing security duty, were continually harassed by Allied artillery fire but no losses were inflicted on them.

On the night from 19 to 20 April, the signals AFV sent to Reference Point 396 changed position to Rosatelli because the boundary of the sector held by the division had been pushed towards the left flank by a distance equal to the width of a battalion.

The birthday of the *Führer,* Adolf Hitler, was celebrated at *Panzer-Abteilung 103,* too. On that particular occasion, the *Kriegsverdienstkreuz* (War Service Cross) was awarded to those who had earned it.

On 21 April *Hauptmann* Heller, the former commander of *2. Kompanie,* arrived. He came to take over the command of *Panzer-Abteilung 103* having been appointed to that post with effect from 15 April. From the same date, *Major* Haen was put on the unattached list of the Supreme High Command of the German Army and was ordered to attend training for staff officers.

On 22 April, the departing commander summoned the staff and line officers of the unit and explained to them that he considered the previous 10 months he had spent as commander of *Panzer-Abteilung 103* a great honour. His *Abteilung* had indeed distinguished itself as the

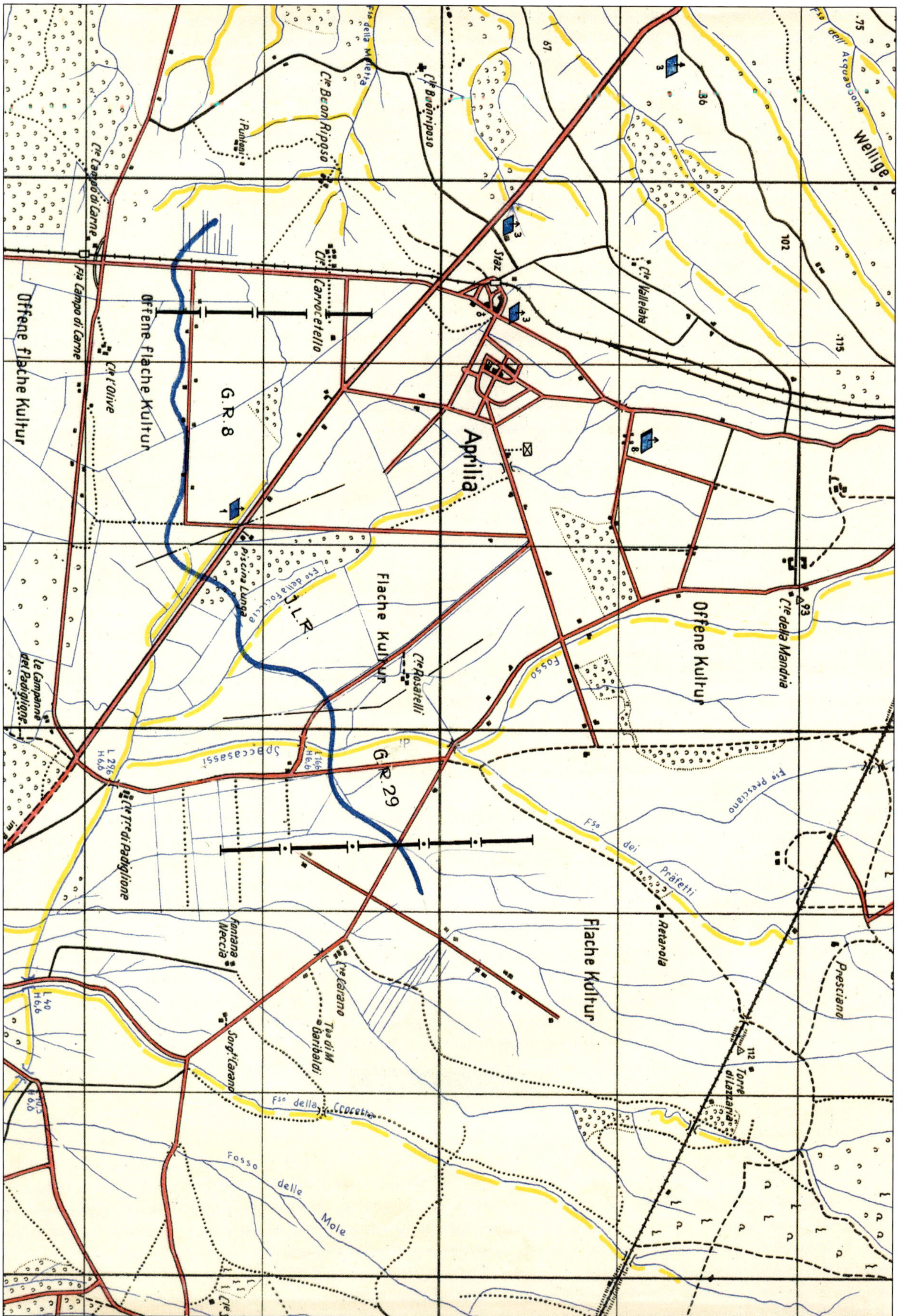

Positions of the StuG. III assault guns of Panzer-Abteilung 103 on 14 April 1944

most outstanding unit of the division and he left behind a combat-ready unit with 42 combat-ready assault guns and a mechanized tank destroyer company for his successor.[159]

By early May the terrain had dried up in the area of the Anzio bridgehead, so the AFVs could be put into action.

The command of the *3. Panzergrenadier-Division* was taken over by *Oberst* Hecker from *Generalleutnant* Gräser, who was transferred to another post. The pioneer's senior officer issued orders to establish the positions of the division in depth. The first line of the defence area extended to the line of the second entrenchment and it was occupied by only one company from each battalion. The second defence zone was Position 'B' which had been established in the area of Aprilia and was defended by two companies of each battalion. This position was to be set up along the northern perimeter of a mine barrage so that it could be observed and placed under fire. The third defence zone – Position 'C' in the area of Ardea – was established 1km further back. Six Tiger E heavy tanks were put into both Positions 'B' and 'C' and an additional three were sent to the railroad running east of Campoleone as a reserve.[160] At that point in time, the acting commander of *Panzer-Abteilung 103* was *Hauptmann der Reserve* Hinzpeter.[161]

On 23 May, American troops launched their break out of the bridgehead and advance in the direction of Rome. From 0840 hours elements of the US 45th Infantry Division pressed home their attack on *Grenadier-Regiment (mot.) 29* on the left flank of the *3. Panzergrenadier-Division* in the area of Carano, and soon the breached the German positions. To clear up the situation, the assault company of the German regiment was put into action together with the *3. Kompanie* of *Panzer-Abteilung 103* while the *5. Kompanie* of *Infanterie-Lehr-Regiment* was also ordered to the area of the breakthrough. With these reinforcements the *III. Bataillon* of *Grenadier-Regiment (mot.) 29* was able to take up new defensive positions at Fso. dei Prefetti and north-east of Point 62 where it successfully prevented the Americans pushing forward across Point 61. During these battles, the battalion received efficient support from the German artillery, as well as from the assault guns of *Panzer-Abteilung 103.*[162]

In the afternoon the American infantry continued its attack with the support of AFVs along the road between Carano and Spacasassi in a north-westerly direction. The *3. Kompanie* of *Grenadier-Regiment (mot.) 29* tried block their progress. The Americans commenced four attacks on the positions of the company but the Germans repelled them, partly in close-combat. The grenadiers were also supported by *Leutnant* Kannengiesser's *3. Kompanie.* During the fighting, one of the StuG. III assault guns was knocked out.[163]

On the left flank of the division the situation became serious because of the disruption of all lines of communication to the *362. Infanterie-Division* which was fighting at the focal point of the attack. As a result, the *3. Panzergrenadier-Division* extended its left flank by putting

---

159 *Kriegstagebuch der Panzer-Abteilung 103* (copy in author's possession), p. 124. The war diary of the unit ends here. No other archival documents of the *3. Panzergrenadier-Division* survived from 1944. Thus the only primary source of information regarding the last months of the fighting in Italy is the *3. Panzergrenadier-Division's* own formal history.

160 Dieckhoff, Gerhard: *3. Infanterie-Division – 3. Infanterie-Division (mot.) – 3. Panzergrenadier-Division* Cuxhaven, s. a., p. 308.

161 Dieckhoff, Gerhard: *3. Infanterie-Division – 3. Infanterie-Division (mot.) – 3. Panzergrenadier-Division* Cuxhaven, s. a., p. 307.

162 Dieckhoff, Gerhard: *3. Infanterie-Division – 3. Infanterie-Division (mot.) – 3. Panzergrenadier-Division* Cuxhaven, s. a., p. 309.

163 Dieckhoff, Gerhard: *3. Infanterie-Division – 3. Infanterie-Division (mot.) – 3. Panzergrenadier-Division* Cuxhaven, s. a., p. 310.

the *1. Kompanie* of *Panzer-Abteilung 103* as well as the *II. Bataillon* of the *Infanterie-Lehr-Regiment* from the divisional reserve into action with the aim of closing the gap between the two divisions at the railroad running towards Tre. di Lazzaria.

On 24 May, *Panzer-Abteilung 103* was drawn forward to Point K18, then its forces were employed separately.

The staff, and probably the *1. Sturmgeschütz-Kompanie*, were put under the command of the *3. Panzergrenadier-Division*; the *2. Sturmgeschütz-Kompanie* (*Oberleutnant* Beschnidt) with the *1. Kompanie* (Elefant heavy tank-destroyers) of *Panzerjäger-Abteilung 653* were assigned to the *362. Infanterie-Division,* and possibly the *3. Sturmgeschütz-Kompanie* with a Tiger company of *schwere Panzer-Abteilung 508* were all fighting under the command of the *715. Infanterie-Division.*[164]

A battle group was set up under the command of *Hauptmann der Reserve* Hinzpeter and this consisted of the *1. Kompanie* of *Panzer-Abteilung 103*, the regimental assault company of *Grenadier-Regiment (mot.) 29,* the *3. Kompanie* of *Pionier-Bataillon (mot.) 3* and elements of divisional *Panzerstörer-Kompanie 3.* They were given the task of preventing the American troops from gaining further ground between the flanks of the *3. Panzergrenadier-Division* and the *362. Infanterie-Division* setting off from the area 1km south-east of Tre. di Presciano, north of the railroad. The battle group linked up with the neighbouring division on the road between Velletri and Cisterna, and then carried out a relief attack from Tre. di Lazzaria in a southerly direction, threatening the flank of the American troops.[165]

In the early hours of the day the *3. Kompanie* of *Panzer-Abteilung 103* was still providing support for the *3. Kompanie* of *Grenadier-Regiment (mot.) 29* along the road running towards Spacasassi. The German company repelled two attacks of company strength. During the fighting the assault guns knocked out a Sherman tank but also lost a StuG. III.[166]

The *2. Kompanie* of *Panzer-Abteilung 103* under command of *Oberleutnant* Beschnidt participated in the defence of Velletri while subordinated to the *362. Infanterie-Division.* For that achievement the officer was later awarded the Knight's Cross of the Iron Cross.[167]

On 25 May, the *14. Armee* intended to reinforce the AT plan of fire at the link-up point between the *362.* and the *715. Infanterie-Division*. For that purpose, an assault gun of *Panzer-Abteilung 103* and eight heavy AT guns of the *4. Fallschirmjäger-Division* were ordered there. By so doing, the assault guns of the company were switched from subordination to the *I. Fallschirm-Korps* to the control of the *LXXVI. Panzerkorps.*[168]

On 27 May the assault guns of *Panzer-Abteilung 103* – probably the *3. Kompanie* – provided support for the *I. Bataillon* of *Grenadier-Regiment (mot.) 29* east of Cavaliere, thereby enabling it to repel an American attack accompanied by six AFVs.[169]

On 29 May at dawn, the *I. Bataillon* of *Grenadier-Regiment (mot.) 29* – reinforced by the *11.* Kompanie of *Grenadier-Regiment (mot.) 8,* two assault guns from the *3. Kompanie* of

164 The German Operation at Anzio. Produced at GMDS by a combined British, Canadian and U.S. Staff, 1946. pp. 108-109.

165 Dieckhoff, Gerhard: *3. Infanterie-Division – 3. Infanterie-Division (mot.) – 3. Panzergrenadier-Division* Cuxhaven, s. a., pp. 310-311.

166 Dieckhoff, Gerhard: *3. Infanterie-Division – 3. Infanterie-Division (mot.) – 3. Panzergrenadier-Division* Cuxhaven, s. a., p. 310.

167 Dieckhoff, Gerhard: *3. Infanterie-Division – 3. Infanterie-Division (mot.) – 3. Panzergrenadier-Division* Cuxhaven, s. a., p. 311.

168 The German Operation at Anzio. Produced at GMDS by a combined British, Canadian and U.S. Staff, 1946. p. 110.

169 Dieckhoff, Gerhard: *3. Infanterie-Division – 3. Infanterie-Division (mot.) – 3. Panzergrenadier-Division*. Cuxhaven, s. a., p. 312.

Geheim

Gültigkeitsliste der K.St.N. und K.A.N. für 3.Pz.Gren.Div.

Truppenteil	Art-Nr.	Datum
1 Kdo./Pz.Gren.Div.	51	1.11.41
1 Div.Kart.St.(mot)	2076 n	1.10.43
Gren.Rgt.(mot):		
2 St. u. St.Kp.Gren.Rgt.(mot)	1104	1.11.43
6 St.Pz.Gren.Btl.	1108	1.11.43
18 Pz.Gren.Kp. b	1114	1.11.43
6 (T.E.) Führ.schw.Kp.(mot)	1121	1.11.43
6 " s.Pz.Jg.Zg.(3 Gesch.)(mot Z)	1145	1.11.43
6 " 12cm Gr.W.Zg.(mot Z) zu 4 Werfern	1126	1.11.43
2 Gesch.Kp. (6 s.I.G. Sf.)	1120 a	1.11.43
2 Gren.Pi.Kp.(mot)	1118 Ausf.A	1.11.43
2 Fla-Kp.(mot S)	192 (gek.)	1. 6.43
Panzer-Aufklärungs-Abt.:		
1 Stb.Pz.Aufkl.Abt.	1109 (gp.)	1.11.43
1 (T.E.)schw.Pz.Spähzug (7,5cm)	1138	1.11.43
1 Pz.-Späh-Kp.	1162	1.11.43
1 Pz.-Späh-Kp. c	1162 c	1.11.43
2 Pz.Aufkl.Kp.(gp.)	1113 (gp.)	1.11.43
1 (T.E.) Führ.schw.Kp.(gp.)	1121a(gp.)	1.11.43
1 " Gesch.Zug a 2 le I.G.(gp.)	1123a(gp.)	1.11.43
1 " Pi.-Zug a (gp.)	1124a(gp.)	1.11.43
1 " schw.Kan.Zug (7,5cm)	1125 (gp.)	1.11.43
1 " schw.Pz.Jg.Zug (3 Gesch.) (gp.)	1145 (gp.)	1.11.43
1 Versorgungs-Kp. Pz.Aufkl.Abt.(gp.)	1180 (gp.)	1.11.43
Pz.-Abt. (Stu.Gesch.)		
1 Stb. Panzer-Abt.	1107	1.11.43
1 Stbskp.(Pz.Stu.Gesch.Abt.(45 Gesch.))	1157 a	1.11.43
3 Pz.Stu.Gesch.Kp.(14 Gesch.)	1159	1.11.43
1 Pz.-Werkst.-Zug	1185 Ausf. A	1. 6.42
Artillerie-Regiment:		
1 Stb.Art.Rgt.(mot)	410	1.11.43
1 Stbsbttr.(mot)Art.Rgt.(mot)	578	1. 1.44
2 Stb.Art.Abt.(mot)	406	1. 1.44
2 Stbsbttr.(mot)Art.Abt.(mot)	586	1. 1.44
3 Bttr.le.F.H.(4 Gesch.)(mot Z)		
2 Bttr. s.F.H.(4 Gesch.)(mot Z)	434	1.11.43
1 Bttr.10cm-Kan.(4 Gesch.)(mot Z)		
1 Stb.Art.Abt.(Sfl.)	407	1.11.43
1 Stbsbttr.Art.Abt.(Sfl.)	583	1.11.43
3 Bttr.le.F.H.(Sfl.)	431	1.11.43
Heeres-Flak-Art.Abt.:		
1 Stb.u.Stbsbttr.(mot) H.Flak-Art.Abt.(mot)	1705	1. 3.44
2 H.Flak-Bttr.8,8cm (4 Gesch.)(mot Z)	1711	1.11.43
1 H.Flak-Bttr. 2cm (12 Gesch.)(mot Z)	1713	1. 1.44
Pionier-Btl.(mot):		
1 Stb.Pi.Btl.(mot) mit Stbskp.(mot)	703	1.11.43
3 Pi.Kp.(mot)	712	1.11.43
1 Brü.Kol.(K)(mot)	737	1.11.43
Nachrichten-Abt.(mot):		
1 Stb.Pz.Gren.Div.Nachr.Abt.	805	1.10.43
1 Pz.Gren.Div.Fsp.Kp.(mot)	832	1.11.43
1 Pz.Gren.Div.Fu.Kp.(mot)	858	1.11.43
1 Div.Nachr.Kol.(mot)	871	1.11.43

List of organizational requirements of the 3. Panzergrenadier-Division's subunits, May 1944

In den ſchweren Kämpfen
im Landekopf Nettuno
ſtarben
für Großdeutſchlands Zukunft:

Lt. Cramme
Lt. Gründel
Lt. Sippell
Lt. Spengler
Lt. Zaunmüller

Stabskompanie

Uffz. Katzke

1. Kompanie

Fw. Bahls
Gefr. Fricke
" Merkl

2. Kompanie

Uffz. Gellrich
Ogefr. Hyra
Gefr. Kandler
" Koſzyk
" Wenzig

3. Kompanie

Ofw. Stockhausen
Uffz. Schwiegershausen
Ogefr. Himmler
Gefr. Derkits
" Melzer
" Leining

List of German soldiers of Panzer-Abteilung 103 killed in action in the Battle of Anzio/Nettuno, January-May 1944

The abandoned StuG. III assault gun '233' from the 2. Kompanie of Panzer-Abteilung 103 in Cori, May 1944

A destroyed StuG. III assault gun of Panzer-Abteilung 103 near Rome, June 1944

Panzer-Abteilung 103, two AT guns and a pioneer platoon acting as infantry – fought severe battles east of La Torretta. According to the war diary of the battalion:

'At 0445 hours sudden but intensifying enemy artillery and mortar fire commences, culminating at around 0500 hours and continuing to come down with undiminished ferocity until 0600 hours. The noise tracks closer and closer and leads us to believe that a major attack with AFV support is imminent. For the time being, defence is impossible.

*Everything happens in the shortest period of time. Visibility has improved, allowing us to notice eight combat vehicles among the positions and an additional seven ferociously firing in front of the main combat line. The enemy infantry is launching its attack. Their reinforcements are continuously carried forward by small armoured vehicles armed with machine guns. The enemy suffers heavy losses in our small arms defensive fire. Our grenadiers are fighting a desperate battle against the massive attack, notwithstanding that each and every anti-tank foxhole is under ferocious fire. There is no tank-destroyer equipment left. The artillery observer lost radio contact and both wire and radio contact with the regiment and with the neighbouring battalions (*III. Bataillon *to the right and assault battalion* 'Genz' *to the left) have also been disrupted. Thus, the battalion is fighting this heavy battle alone.*

[...]

The MG 42 machine guns are scattering a ceaseless hail of bullets into the assaulting mass. One of the tanks is knocked out, followed by another two. The enemy infantry is halted. However, the danger has not passed. Another 12 enemy tanks are still standing among or before our positions.

An additional two assault guns arrive from the III. Bataillon *(to the right) to lend a helping hand. A young* Fahnenjunker-Unteroffizier *knocks out five Shermans in a few minutes. The enemy has no hope of lasting much longer. The* 'Amis' *retreat, panic stricken, to their jump-off positions.'*[170]

The *3. Panzergrenadier-Division* was still holding Position 'C' plus a blocking position at Lanuvio on that day. In the sector of the German division about 200 Allied AFVs attacked, of which 15 were knocked. Including these, the forces of the division had reported a total of 62 knocked-out enemy AFVs during the offensive commenced on 23 May.[171]

On the same day, *Oberfeldwebel* Fritz Scherf, a platoon commander from the *2. Kompanie* of *Panzer-Abteilung 103* was killed. He was posthumously awarded the Knight's Cross of the Iron Cross – in recognition of the 42 enemy AFVs knocked out by him – on 30 September 1944.[172]

On 30 May, while providing support for the *I. Bataillon* of *Fallschirmjäger-Regiment 11,* the assault guns of *Panzer-Abteilung 103* knocked out two Allied AFVs in the area of Cle. Pasquali.

The *I. Bataillon* of *Grenadier-Regiment (mot.) 29* was supported by only two StuG. IIIs from the *3. Kompanie* of *Panzer-Abteilung 103.* However, one of them was knocked out by the Allies.[173]

On 31 May, at the connecting point between the *I.* and *II. Bataillone* of *Grenadier-Regiment (mot.) 29,* 15 Allied AFVs broke through with infantry shuttled on the top of them. The *1.*

170 Dieckhoff, Gerhard: 3. Infanterie-Division – *3. Infanterie-Division (mot.) – 3. Panzergrenadier-Division* Cuxhaven, s. a., p. 315.

171 Dieckhoff, Gerhard: 3. Infanterie-Division – *3. Infanterie-Division (mot.) – 3. Panzergrenadier-Division* Cuxhaven, s. a., p. 315.

172 Dieckhoff, Gerhard: 3. Infanterie-Division – *3. Infanterie-Division (mot.) – 3. Panzergrenadier-Division* Cuxhaven, s. a., p. 417.

173 Dieckhoff, Gerhard: *3. Infanterie-Division – 3. Infanterie-Division (mot.) – 3. Panzergrenadier-Division* Cuxhaven, s. a., p. 316.

Kompanie of the regiment repulsed them in close combat and disabled two combat vehicles by using *Panzerfaust* anti-tank weapons. The assault guns of the *3. Kompanie* of *Panzer-Abteilung 103* scored another three knock-outs. Later the StuG. IIIs gave support in repelling the attack launched on the *III. Bataillon* and, having eliminated the breach, then joined forces and retook the previous positions.[174]

On that day the following combat-ready German armoured force (33 tanks and 47 assault guns) engaged the Allied troops that had broken out of the Anzio bridgehead:

- *Fallschirm-Sturmgeschütz-Brigade 11* with three tanks and 22 Italian-made assault guns;
- *65. Infanterie-Division* with an Italian-made assault guns;
- *3. Panzergrenadier-Division* with 15 StuG. III assault guns of *Panzer-Abteilung 103;*
- *Panzer-Division 'Hermann Göring'* with 20 tanks and seven assault guns;
- *schwere Panzer-Abteilung 508* with 10 Tiger E heavy tanks;
- *1. Kompanie* of *schwere Panzerjäger-Abteilung 653* with two Elefant tank destroyers.[175]

During the day's fighting four German assault guns were destroyed by receiving hits from the Allied artillery.[176]

On 4 July, the remainder of the *3. Panzergrenadier-Regiment* established new defensive positions north of Rome. According to eyewitness accounts, one Elefant tank destroyer and two or three assault guns were among the last troops to leave the Eternal City which was not defended by the Germans.[177] In connection with the assault guns mentioned, it cannot be excluded that these were StuG. IIIs of *Panzer-Abteilung 103.*

During the holding manoeuvres here, the assault guns of *Panzer-Abteilung 103* and the pioneers from *Pionier-Bataillon (mot.) 3* excelled themselves. Their achievements were even mentioned in the daily reports of the *Wehrmacht.*[178]

In the course of the retreat, *Panzer-Abteilung 103,* under the command of *Hauptmann* Heller and *Hauptmann der Reserve* Hinzpeter, provided continuous support for their own infantry, repaired its damaged assault guns immediately behind the front line and then put them into action again. The armoured unit itself lost very few written-off tanks during the fighting withdrawal, but knocked out more than 30 Allied AFVs.[179]

---

174 Dieckhoff, Gerhard: *3. Infanterie-Division – 3. Infanterie-Division (mot.) – 3. Panzergrenadier-Division* Cuxhaven, s. a., p. 317.

175 The German Operation at Anzio. Produced at GMDS by a combined British, Canadian and U.S. Staff, 1946. p. 118.

176 The German Operation at Anzio. Produced at GMDS by a combined British, Canadian and U.S. Staff, 1946. p. 119.

177 Dieckhoff, Gerhard: *3. Infanterie-Division – 3. Infanterie-Division (mot.) – 3. Panzergrenadier-Division* Cuxhaven, s. a., p. 319.

178 Dieckhoff, Gerhard: 3. *Infanterie-Division – 3. Infanterie-Division (mot.) – 3. Panzergrenadier-Division* Cuxhaven, s. a., p. 322.

179 NARA T312, R487 (*Armeeoberkommando 14*), F8079053.

6

Holding manoeuvres up to the River Arno

After the Allies forced the German troops out of the positions they had established south of Rome, the next sector suitable for permanent defence, the so-called Position 'Green' (*Grün-Stellung* in German) stretched 280km north of the Italian capital. The system of positions, established 35km north of the River Arno, was built across the Italian peninsula from Viareggio to Pesaro. It was known as the 'Gothic Line' by the Allies. Leaving rear guard detachments with considerable firepower behind, they tried to reach that new line in successive echelons as soon as possible.

The *3. Panzergrenadier-Division* had been considerably weakened in the battles fought for the Anzio Bridgehead and retreated 75km between 5 and 9 June 1944. In the area of Lake Bolsena the battle strength of the division was only 1,000 men.[180]

On 10 June, 20 new StuG. IIIs were issued to *Panzer-Abteilung 103.*[181] The AFVs were dispatched from Firenze via Siena.[182]

On the night from 13 to 14 June, the division was withdrawn to the containing positions established in the area of Acquapendete. *Panzer-Abteilung 103* had two command combat vehicles and seven StuG. III assault guns combat-ready at that time.[183]

From 16 June German forces carried out holding manoeuvres and the pace of their retreat decreased to about 2km per day.[184]

On 17 June, in the evening, *Panzer-Abteilung 103* possessed 27 combat-ready assault guns.[185] By that time, the material losses of the workshop platoon had amounted to 50%.[186]

By 20 June, most of the newly arrived assault guns had broken down due to the marches carried out inexpertly and impetuously.[187]

180 Dieckhoff, Gerhard: 3. Infanterie-Division – 3. Infanterie-Division (mot.) – 3. Panzergrenadier-*Division* Cuxhaven, s. a., p. 321.
181 NARA T312, R488 (*Armeeoberkommando 14*), F8080152.
182 NARA T312, R486 (*Armeeoberkommando 14*), F8077428.
183 NARA T312, R487 (*Armeeoberkommando 14*), F8079041.
184 Dieckhoff, Gerhard: *3. Infanterie-Division – 3. Infanterie-Division (mot.) – 3. Panzergrenadier-Division* Cuxhaven, s. a., p. 326.
185 NARA T312, R487 (*Armeeoberkommando 14*), F8079025. It is highly possible that the new assault guns issued had also arrived by that time.
186 NARA T312, R486 (*Armeeoberkommando 14*), F8077434.
187 NARA T312, R486 (*Armeeoberkommando 14*), F8077436.

On 22 June, *Panzer-Abteilung 103* had a total of 37 assault guns but only seven StuG. IIIs were combat-ready. The armoured unit was on march back to the sector of the *3. Panzergrenadier-Division.*[188]

On the night from 28 to 29 June the forces of the *3. Panzergrenadier-Division* reached the southern foreground of Monteguidi during their retreat. There, the combat-ready forces of the division were subordinated to the *20. Felddivision* of the *Luftwaffe.* The divisional staff marched to the area of Carmignano to prepare the reorganization and reinforcement of the division to bring it back up to strength.[189] The commander of the *III. Bataillon* of *Grenadier-Regiment (mot.) 8, Hauptmann* Weck gives the following account of the defence of Monteguidi:

'On 29 June in the evening the situation at my battalion was as follows: the company of Leutnant *Clever (10./8) linking up with* Grenadier-Regiment 956 (362. Infanterie-Division) *to the right occupied the highest point on the Casaccia Ridge with their general front line southwards. Two mortars and a rifle section were put into action under command of* Oberleutnant *Meyer from [company] 'Gottesberge' (9./8) 800m south of the cemetery of Monteguidi with the task of covering the flank to the left. An attached AT gun platoon and an assault gun platoon were sent northwards because the only route for retreat was threatened. I moved the battalion command post to Monteguidi shortly after midnight (on 30 June).*

[…]

To the left, at 1015 hours, six enemy AFVs were observed with accompanying infantry of company strength on the east-west road immediately south of Mensano making rapid progress westward. However the first AFV, having reached the road fork 1km west of Mensano at 1030 hours, turned in a northerly direction towards Casole d'Elsa. Thus the danger threatening to the left was temporarily eliminated.

At around 1300 hours, about 30 AFVs started off on their march from the valley of [the River] Cecina in a northerly and north-easterly direction. However they stopped 1500m from Monteguidi. It was evident that the AFVs had been given the task to secure the crossing and to prepare for the infantry marching across the river without a moment's rest. The securing AFVs and the infantry marching across the Cecina were taken under efficient fire by the artillery and the Nebelwerfers. *However it was far too weak to prevent the enemy from moving.*

The situation at the road fork had changed in the following way: the effective fire (probably from our own assault guns) set an AFV on fire and disabled another one. Upon that, the enemy AFVs retreated to the road fork.'[190]

On 2 July the combat elements of the *3. Panzergrenadier-Division* were pulled out of the front line. At that time *Panzer-Abteilung 103* had a total of eight combat-ready StuG. III assault guns left. Their number was successfully boosted to 14 combat-ready assault guns,

188 NARA T312, R486 (*Armeeoberkommando 14*), F8078095.

189 Dieckhoff, Gerhard: *3. Infanterie-Division – 3. Infanterie-Division (mot.) – 3. Panzergrenadier-Division* Cuxhaven, s. a., p. 323.

190 Dieckhoff, Gerhard: *3. Infanterie-Division – 3. Infanterie-Division (mot.) – 3. Panzergrenadier-Division* Cuxhaven, s. a., p. 324.

Two StuG. III assault guns out of action from Panzer-Abteilung 103
in an unknown location, summer 1944

although the AFVs were to hand part of their machine guns over to the infantry of the division.[191]

During the next two days, the AFVs of *Panzer-Abteilung 103* were repaired – also by *Panzerkampfwagen-Werkstatt-Kompanie 929.*[192]

On 7 July, the division received orders to relieve the *20. Felddivision* of the *Luftwaffe* two days later. The *3. Panzergrenadier-Division* was allocated to a 13km wide sector between the north-south valleys of the Rivers Era and Elsa. However, the Allies exerted most of their pressure elsewhere. The *1. Kompanie* of *Panzer-Abteilung 103* (*Oberleutnant* Schwäpenheuer) was employed on the right flank together with the Wespe self-propelled howitzers of the *1. Batterie* of *Artillerie-Regiment (mot.) 3.*

The *2. Sturmgeschütz-Kompanie* (*Oberleutnant* Beschnidt) provided support for *Jäger-Regiment 40* of the *Luftwaffe* in the middle, in the area of Montignoso. On the left flank, the *3. Sturmgeschütz-Kompanie* (*Oberleutnant* Geisser) was fighting in cooperation with elements of *Grenadier-Regiment (mot.) 29.*[193]

On 12 July, *Panzer-Abteilung 103* had a total of 32 StuG. III assault guns, of which 19 were combat-ready.[194]

On 13 July, in the afternoon the *1. Sturmgeschütz-Kompanie* took the attacking Allied troops in the flank with the support of the German artillery south and south-west of Barbialla. Under the cover of the falling night, the Allies decided to retreat.

On 23 July, in the morning, in the area of San Miniato, *Grenadier-Regiment (mot.) 8* were forced to eliminate an Allied breach without the support of the assault guns because they were unable to bypass detonations on the road.

On 25 July, the *3. Kompanie* of *Panzer-Abteilung 103*, in cooperation with the forces of *Grenadier-Regiment (mot.) 29* as well as those of the *III. Abteilung* and the *2. Batterie* of *Artillerie-Regiment (mot.) 3*, fought in the Florence Bridgehead. By the following dawn the bridgehead had been pulled back eastwards.

On 26 July, violent battles were fought for the bridgehead. *Panzer-Abteilung 103* with 14 combat ready assault guns and a company of *Grenadier-Regiment (mot.) 29* successfully blocked the Allied troops that had penetrated the bridgehead in the area of Ginestra. The front line of the division was pulled back to the line of the River Pesa.[195]

On the night from 31 July to 1 August, the elements of the *3. Panzergrenadier-Division* were already fighting on the northern bank of the River Arno but *Grenadier-Regiment (mot.) 8*, reinforced by the *2.* and *3. Kompanie* of *Panzer-Abteilung 103*, still held a bridgehead south of the river.

By dawn, 3 August, the Germans had evacuated the southern bank of the River Arno almost completely, but the forces put into action there as a rear guard – the *II. Bataillon* of

191 Dieckhoff, Gerhard: *3. Infanterie-Division – 3. Infanterie-Division (mot.) – 3. Panzergrenadier-Division* Cuxhaven, s. a., p. 326.
192 NARA T312, R486 (*Armeeoberkommando 14*), F8077191 and F8077193.
193 Dieckhoff, Gerhard: *3. Infanterie-Division – 3. Infanterie-Division (mot.) – 3. Panzergrenadier-Division* Cuxhaven, s. a., p. 327.
194 NARA T312, R490 (*Armeeoberkommando 14*), F8082929.
195 Dieckhoff, Gerhard: *3. Infanterie-Division – 3. Infanterie-Division (mot.) – 3. Panzergrenadier-Division* Cuxhaven, s. a., p. 329.

Grenadier-Regiment (mot.) 8 and the assault guns of *Leutnant* Göb – crossed the river and reached the northern bank only on the following day.[196]

During the next two weeks, the Allies temporarily ceased attacking with significant forces because they had to wait for the signals and engineering units to close up and their troops were in need of artillery ammunition. The Germans used that lull in the fighting to reinforce their temporary positions.

The *1. Kompanie* of *Panzer-Abteilung 103* and the *6. Kompanie* of *Grenadier-Regiment (mot.) 29* were amalgamated into a single battle group to close the motorway running between Florence and Pistoia if needed.

The armoured unit of the *3. Panzergrenadier-Division* already had 27 combat-ready StuG. IIIs at that time, which were partly received as repaired vehicles from the workshop platoon and partly as newly issued ones.[197]

On 16 August, the division received orders to retreat from the front line.

On 18 August by 1600 hours, the troops had been relieved by elements of the *362. Infanterie-Division.*

On 20 August the last couple of assault guns of *Panzer-Abteilung 103,* still performing security duty, were pulled out of their positions. On that day it turned out that the division would be sent into action in another theatre, on the Western Front. Although the troops handed over their remaining Wespe self-propelled howitzers to their comrades still fighting in Italy, we cannot read the same about the assault guns in the history of the division.[198]

196 Dieckhoff, Gerhard: *3. Infanterie-Division – 3. Infanterie-Division (mot.) – 3. Panzergrenadier-Division* Cuxhaven, s. a., p. 329.

197 Dieckhoff, Gerhard: *3. Infanterie-Division – 3. Infanterie-Division (mot.) – 3. Panzergrenadier-Division* Cuxhaven, s. a., p. 330.

198 Dieckhoff, Gerhard: 3. Infanterie-Division – 3. Infanterie-Division (mot.) – 3. Panzergrenadier-*Division* Cuxhaven, s. a., p. 330.